Keep the Home Fires Burning

The Hull area in the First World War

This book belongs to

Victoria Wheater

Highgate Publications (Beverley) Ltd
1988

Published by Highgate Publications (Beverley) Ltd.
24 Wylies Road, Beverley, HU17 7AP
Telephone (0482) 866826

Printed and Typeset in 10 on 11pt Plantin by
B.A. Press, 2-4 Newbegin, Lairgate, Beverley, HU17 8EG
Telephone (0482) 882232

ISBN 0 948929 14 6

British Library Cataloguing in Publication Data

Keep The Home Fires Burning: the Hull area in the First World War.
   1. Humberside. Hull — 1910-1936.
   I. Markham, John.
     942.8'37083

ISBN 0-948929-14-6

Cover picture — After the raid on Edwin Davis's [G. Michael Kilvington]

FOREWORD

To a generation raised under the threat of global war and total annihilation, the enthusiasm with which people in the United Kingdom welcomed the outbreak of war in 1914 is a continuing source of bewilderment. In retrospect, this misplaced eagerness to fight reflected the extent to which war, fighting and, indeed, service in the military, had been alien to the man on the Victorian and Edwardian Clapham omnibus. Throughout the period, men and women had enjoyed the benefits of *Pax Britannica*. The navy and army were unknown institutions. Most of the army were serving overseas in postings which ranged from Bermuda to the Cape and from Nova Scotia to Mauritius. The navy ruled the seas, its dreadnoughts, cruiser squadrons and new-fangled torpedo-boat destroyers reflecting the might of British imperialism. And where those troops did fight, they were engaged in a succession of colonial campaigns. When the regiments were successful, the public at home basked in the reflected glory. 'By the side of the immense slaughter of dervishes', wrote Steevens in his account of the Battle of Omdurman in 1898, 'the tale of our casualties is so small as to be almost ridiculous'. Even defeats could be glorified. The successful defence of Rorke's Drift in 1879 by just over one hundred men was a favourable topic remembered in excruciating verse by Edmund Pertwee and in a slightly superior painting by Lady Elizabeth Butler. Henty, Kipling, Winter and Henley created an image of military life which in its stress on patriotism, glory and honour, ill prepared a public for the realities of twentieth-century warfare.

The four years from 1914 onwards were thus cruel years. In the beginning, men rushed to enlist, fearful that it would all be over even before they had seen action. In the end, they feared they never would escape from the mud and carnage that was Flanders. Locked into trench warfare, eye-deep in hell, officers and men created their own memories of the world that they once had known. One of the cruellest features of this war was the nearness of that world in geographical terms and its distance in attainability. Yet it was not entirely the world of that glorious summer of 1914. For the civilian, too, it was a cruel time. As push after push failed, War Office telegrams were delivered in increasing numbers. In some streets of Hull the grim announcements of substantial casualty lists brought home to almost every house the harsh realities of the slaughter of the trenches. Village war memorials today recapture in chiselled stone the anguish and heartbreak faced by rural families. Nor was the pain suffered by civilians only a mental anguish. For the first time in the United Kingdom, new instruments of war brought death to men, women and children alike. In Scarborough, civilians were shelled; in Hull, they suffered from the bombs dropped by slim silver Zeppelins whose elegant silhouette against the night sky belied the pain and destruction they carried with them.

It is with this world that John Markham is concerned. Much has been written on the First World War but the *local* impact of those years has not received the attention which it deserves. It is only when one has the opportunity to read a book such as this that the full extent of this effect can readily be appreciated. By drawing extensively in Part One on accounts of local newspapers, John has been able to demonstrate very readily the manner in which our predecessors in Hull and the East Riding sought to accommodate, and respond to, the effect on their lives of a truly traumatic experience. For one family — the Hohenreins — the difficulties of these four years were particularly poignant. But for all those ordinary people — the men and women on the Anlaby tram — whose experiences are recounted in the third part of this book, the years of 1914-18 were an unparalleled and unprecedented experience. These were the people who kept the home fires burning; they, together with their colleagues throughout what is now Humberside, provided that image of British society which, for so many who fought in that war, was the difference between the insanity of war and the logic of normality. It is this image which John Markham brings out so vividly in this book.

October, 1988.   GWYN HARRIES-JENKINS
                                            Dean, School of Adult
                                            and Continuing Education,
                                            University of Hull.

PREFACE

Anyone who has experienced a war knows that it is a time of oddly mixed emotions, when appalling tragedy is relieved by interludes of unexpected joy. Great events jostle with the trivia of everyday life and the ordinary takes on a special significance. This book is an impressionistic survey of the home front in the Hull area during the First World War. Its aim is to capture the atmosphere of four emotion-charged years, not to provide a detailed chronological study. Historians need two particular attributes: accuracy and imagination. The first is difficult enough to achieve, and the second depends on so many personal factors that no one can claim to have re-created the past as it really was. If fleeting glimpses of truth occur, I shall consider my selection of material vindicated.

Part One consists of a variety of extracts from local newspapers, which convey the flavour of the time more potently than most other sources of information. Part Two focuses on a family mentioned in the newspapers, the Hohenreins, and Part Three is based on the recollections of 'ordinary people' who did not feature in the press but whose experiences represent those of the greater part of the population.

The phrase, 'the Hull area', in the sub-title needs explanation. Most of the contents of this book relate to Hull, but to provide a fuller picture there are a number of references to other local villages and towns. The interviews conducted by Peter Adamson's students took place on both sides of the Humber (though some interviewees, as he explains, were elsewhere during the Great War). It would have been convenient to use the concise title, Humberside, to define the area largely covered by this book, but purists would have objected to such a name as an anachronism. Consequently the less precise but, I believe, still reasonable sub-title has been selected — without apology!

I have been considerably helped in the editing of this book by the kind cooperation of many people and I wish to express my gratitude to these and, in particular, to thank:

The County Librarian and Humberside Libraries and Arts for permission to reproduce material from the collection in the Local Studies Library, Central Library, Hull, and, in addition, the staff of that library and of the Beverley Reference Library for help on many occasions; Hull City Museums and Art Galleries for permission to reproduce photographs from the collection at the Town Docks Museum; Christopher Ketchell for permission to reproduce illustrations from his collection; Mr. G. Michael Kilvington for the kind loan of the book, 'Zeppelin Raids on Hull 1915-1918', compiled by his late father, Chief Superintendent C. B. Kilvington, C.I.D., and for permission to reproduce photographs therefrom; Peter Adamson for his kind cooperation in providing transcripts of interviews with senior citizens; Joe Brown for his skilful editing of the transcripts; Mrs. Wright for permission to reproduce the essay by her husband, Mr. Leonard M. Wright; Her Majesty's Stationery Office for permission to reproduce Crown Copyright material; My colleagues, Irene and Martyn Kirby, for their continuing support and unfailing kindness; and Barry Sage and the B.A. Press for their amazing willingness to cooperate with Highgate's requests to complete work on our books in such unreasonably short periods.

October, 1988.   John Markham

Part One

WHAT THE PAPERS SAID

The First World War through the columns of local newspapers

    (a)   The outbreak of war — 4 August, 1914

    (b)   The Home Front. The Zeppelin raid on Hull, 6 June, 1915 — and the aftermath

    (c)   Peace — 11 November, 1918

Abbreviations used:

BG — *Beverley Guardian*
EMN — *Eastern Morning News*
HDM — *Hull Daily Mail*

The outbreak of war — 4 August, 1914

It promised to be another beautiful August Bank Holiday weekend in a beautiful summer, and older people who remember the years before the First World War are convinced that the weather has never been so good again.

The Bank Holiday was then at the beginning of the month — 3 August — and extra trains had been arranged to take the expected thousands of day-trippers to the seaside to enjoy a stroll along the front at Withernsea, Hornsea or Bridlington, to escape for a few blessed hours the stifling streets of Hull. Families from the crowded terraces were looking forward to the breath of sea air which always did them a world of good : better, many claimed, than the Carter's Little Liver Pills, Dr. Williams' Pink Pills, or Bile Beans which, according to the regular advertisements in the papers, could do marvellous things.

From their carriage windows, trippers in August, 1914, could observe and pass favourable comments on the fields of corn fast ripening for the harvest. Village schools broke up for the holidays even later than they do today and everyone spoke of the 'harvest holidays', for children were needed to help the grown-ups in the busy autumn fields.

Suddenly the mood changed. The gloomy news from abroad refused to go away and became more and more worrying, showers dampened the spirits of day trippers who had been determined to go to the seaside, despite the cancellation of the excursion trains, and, after a tense Bank Holiday, war was declared on Tuesday, 4 August, and a way of life came to an end. Things would never be the same again; for once, the cliché was right. It was the end of the old world and the beginning of a new. Luckily, that weekend few realised how terrible this new world would be. Edward Grey, the Foreign Secretary, was one of the few with prophetic vision. 'The lights are going out all over Europe,' he said; 'we shall not see them lit again in our lifetime.'

Local newspapers reflect most vividly the impact of war on the people of the area. One minute they are filled with the customary reports of births, marriages and deaths, cricket matches, and the shows at the Alexandra, the Grand, the Palace and the Tivoli, the films at Princes Hall, 'The Home of Electric Theatres', the amateur performances of *The Mikado* in Withernsea, and all the nostalgic trivia it is such a pleasure to read. Then the ominous black headlines appear, and other events intrude : men enlisting, Territorials recalled from their summer camp, the crowds at Paragon

Wenlock Barracks, Hull.   [Christopher Ketchell Collection]

Concert Party.   [Christopher Ketchell Collection]

Station, not always managing to keep a stiff upper lip as their menfolk went off to do their duty to King and Country.

The emotional intensity of these newspaper reports is all the greater because it is unintended and understated, written in the sedate, mannered style of well-rounded sentences, displaying the perfect syntax then demanded of every journalist. Only a modern reader with the benefit of hindsight knows the rest of the story and can see poignancy and pathos in the advertisements of the programmes of the band concerts in Pearson and Pickering Parks, for Field's Café, and for the splendid new houses in Anlaby Park, the lingering signs of everyday life, printed with tragic incongruity among the news from Serbia, Berlin and London.

———————

Bank Holiday Monday, 3 August, 1914

This morning opens fair and fresh, one of the loveliest days we have had this beautiful season, but our holidaymakers find themselves without the accustomed cheap facilities for getting to distant scenes, the trains being required for the transport of troops.

(HDM)

North-Eastern Railway
Withdrawal of Excursions

The North-Eastern Railway Company regret to announce that they have been compelled to CANCEL ALL EXCURSIONS advertised to run from North-Eastern Stations for

Sunday August 2

Monday August 3 and

Tuesday August 4

A. Kaye Butterworth

York 2nd August General Manager

(HDM)

4th East Yorks Regiment — Men will attend at Londesborough Barracks and East Hull at 5 p.m. to receive orders — W.T. Wilkinson, Captain and Adjutant 4th East Yorks.

(HDM)

East Riding Territorials

Colonel Lambert White presided on Wednesday over a meeting of the East Riding Territorial Association at the Guildhall, Hull. The chairman remarked, in respect to the supply of clothing for the Army Reservists, that 500 uniforms would be ready within the next few days.

(BG)

We Will Stand By Belgium

If the German soldiery crosses the frontier, not only will our national safety be menaced but our sacred obligations will be traversed. A pistol will have been pointed at the heart of England and an insult put upon us by the thought that we should stand idly by.

(HDM)

Hornsea

Disbanded Camp. The West Riding Divisional Royal Engineers arrived on Sunday at mid-day by special train, and detrained at the Bridge Station for the Southorpe Road camping ground for 14 days' training. A large crowd of visitors and residents assembled at the station to give them a welcome, the number of men arriving being about 500, with 120 horses. The camping ground was open to the public, and during the afternoon and evening a good number of visitors attended. On Monday morning news arrived that the camp had to be struck and the men returned to headquarters, and they left Hornsea by special train at 4.30 p.m. that day.

(BG)

Hull Territorials Brought Home From Camp
Scenes at the Barracks

The 4th East Yorkshire Regiment arrived home this morning, weary with their exertions, but they received orders to be back again at the

A typical picture. The family has not been identified but the uniform is an East Yorkshire one, probably a 'Commercial'.
[Christopher Ketchell Collection]

Londesborough Barracks, and also at East Hull, at 5 p.m. to receive orders. They were also ordered to be prepared for a journey to another town. The Royal Field Artillery, Wenlock Barracks, Anlaby Road, left Dundee Camp yesterday afternoon at 5 o'clock and did not reach Hull until about 10 o'clock this morning. All the men were fatigued, some of them not having had a meal since they entrained yesterday afternoon. When they arrived at the Barracks about noon there was a crowd of mothers, sweethearts and friends waiting, some of them having been there since 10 a.m. But they were destined to have a long wait, for the soldiers were not allowed to leave the Barracks for nearly two hours, the officers stating that they must wait in case an Army Order arrived.

(HDM)

Hurrying Home
400 Trawlers Coming to Port
Striking Scene in Humber

The fishing trawlers belonging to Hull have been ordered home and are hurrying to get into port for protection. The Humber presented a striking picture today. There were, when the *Mail* paid a visit early in the afternoon, about a hundred trawlers anchored in the river. These included the major portions of the Red Cross and Hellyers' Fleets and, as they occupied the stretch of water from off the Fish Dock, they looked something like a huge torpedo boat flotilla.

(HDM)

Middleton Garden Party

Owing to the terrible national crisis it has been decided to give the proceeds of the Garden Party at Middleton Hall next Tuesday partly to the Red Cross and partly to some fund for the relief of those families whose bread-winners are fighting. The entertainments cannot be on such a big scale as originally intended, but it is much hoped friends and neighbours will attend.

(BG)

Local Food Situation

There is some probability — but no immediate cause for concern — of a scarcity of sugar in Hull. This is owing to the non-arrival this weekend of additional supplies. The Wilson liner *Castro* from Danzig, which has a large quantity of sugar on board, has been detained by the Germans at Hamburg . . .

The Hull fruit trade has been seriously affected. At the time of writing only Dutch and Ghent steamers had arrived, but the *Aaro*, which also brings some fruit, is due to arrive this midday ... The Riverside Quay, which is usually stacked with fruit at this time, presents a naked appearance. No steamer has left Hamburg, from whence a large quantity of fruit comes to Hull, since Wednesday.

(HDM)

Field's Café
Market Place
Tomorrow's Luncheon-Room Menu
12 — 2.30 p.m.

Tomato and Oxtail Soups
Boiled Halibut and Parsley Sauce
Filleted Plaice and Anchovy Sauce
Fried Whiting and Anchovy Sauce
Fish Cakes
Roast Duck and Apple Sauce
Boiled Chicken and White Sauce
Stewed Steak and Carrots
Boiled Bacon and Broad Beans
Lamb Fry
Veal and Ham Pie
Haricot Oxtail
Steak and Kidney Pie
Steak and Kidney Pudding
Vienna Steak and Fried Onions
Stewed Cutlets and Peas
Rissoles and Potatoes
Chop and Chips   Steak and Chips
Roast Chine of Beef
Roast Leg of Lamb and Mint Sauce
Stuffed Fillet of Veal
Vegetables   Sweets etc

Popular Prices

(HDM)

Effect on Hull Shipping

No vessels left the docks by this morning's tide, and there was only one arrival, the Wilson liner *Kyno* from Riga, with a general cargo, entering Victoria Dock.

(HDM)

The Wilson liner *Volpino* has reached Grimsby today from Christiansand. She had not been heard of for several days and her arrival caused considerable anxiety.

(HDM)

Field Kitchen. [Christopher Ketchell Collection]

154, Walker Street Hull: An incendiary bomb fell through the roof on to the landing. The fire was extinguished by the occupants, Mr. and Mrs. Scott, 6 June, 1915.

[Hull City Museums and Art Galleries]

Grimsby Flour Panic

There was a mad rush on the part of many householders to purchase flour and hosts of the small tradesmen were quickly sold out ... As a result of the demand the wholesale price was advanced to 40s. per 20-stone sack, being an increase in price of 13s. per sack within a week.

(HDM)

In Church and Chapel
(i) King's Hall Resolution
[A large Methodist church, built in 1910, in Fountain Road.]

The following resolution was passed at King's Hall, yesterday:

'The members of the King's Hall Brotherhood and Sisterhood and people's services view with horror the terrible outrage to humanity and the menacing challenge to Christianity involved in European war.

They desire to strengthen by every means in their power the strenuous efforts which Great Britain is making for limiting the area of conflict, maintaining our own peaceful relations with the nations of Europe and preserving our freedom to act for peace as opportunity offers.'

(HDM)

(ii) Archbishop of York's Weighty Words
[in a sermon preached the previous day in York Minster]

There must be no hint, no word, no movement in the direction of party, no class advantage. The whole people must rally round the King and his Ministers.

(HDM)

(iii) Newland Congregational Church

Rev. J.G. Patton: 'The first lesson they must take to heart was that Europe was one in all her interests, including government, industrial, social and religious independence. What was required was to work for the establishment of a great European central government for the unification of the government of Europe.

(HDM)

Anxiety in Hull
Men leave for Duty
(Special for the *Daily Mail*)

The people of Hull are watching the march of events with keen anxiety. How deep it is was shown by the crowd which filled Whitefriargate yesterday, waiting for the news as it came through. [The *Hull Daily Mail* and *Eastern Morning News* offices were in Whitefriargate.] As a port of considerable strategic importance, Hull is realising what far reaching effects even the alarms of war mean ...

At the shipping office in Posterngate there were scenes which show what the patriotism of the Englishman is. Royal Naval Reserve men in their uniforms were responding to the call and signing on ... wiry, hard-looking sailors they mostly seemed, their Jack Tar garments not quite at home on their forms. They all carried their kit, a pillow-case-like package with a few changes, shaving tackle and rug. A few of the womenfolk came with some of them and they looked rather anxious.

(HDM)

Fitting Up The 'Terriers'
Horses and Motors Commandeered

There were stirring scenes at the Corporation Field all last night and this morning. The 5th (Cyclists) Battalion East Yorkshire Regiment had been detained under the mobilisation order at the barracks last night, and until 3 a.m. this morning there was a medical examination of the men. After they had been examined the men slept on the ground underneath the shed in Corporation Field and resumed their active preparations this morning. They breakfasted in the open and detachments were sent into the city to commandeer extra cycles. Later there was a test of motor vans that had been taken from their owners under martial law, and those unable to pass the military test were sent back ...

Animated scenes were witnessed at the Paragon Station. During the morning three or four hundred reservists of the Regular Army left for Chatham and other depots to join their regiments. So great were the crowds inside and outside that the gates were closed and people were only admitted by ticket ...

Under the martial law now prevailing tradesmen will have to suffer the loss of horses, motors, etc. .. One of the many incidents which occurred by the order happened at Carr Lane livery stables. A certain doctor's horse and carriage was just leaving when two army officers ordered the horse to be taken out as they needed it for war purposes.

(HDM)

Yorkshire Farm Waggoners Reserve Called Up

The Yorkshire Farm Waggoners Special Reserve numbering close on 1,000, which were raised two or three years ago by Sir Mark Sykes, M.P., were mobilised on Thursday, and a large number left Malton. With their knowledge of East Yorkshire roads they will be of great use as transport drivers.

Their mobilisation in face of the harvest is a serious blow to farmers, who will be short-handed, and harvest as a consequence will be retarded.

(BG)

Three Palace Artistes 'Called Up'

Even music halls are affected by the war. The Three Aeros, trapeze artistes, were to appear at the Palace last evening but could not keep their engagement as they had been called for military service.

(HDM)

Pathetic Hull Station Scenes

About 100 naval reservists left Hull for the south of England on the 5.5 train for London. There were pathetic scenes as the train left. The sailors steadied their nerves and said 'Goodbye' to wives and children.

(HDM)

Hull Priest Leaves to Fight the Germans

Father Leclerc, Chaplain of the Endsleigh Convent, left Hull this morning at 9 o'clock to join the 13th French Regiment. He will endeavour to get to France by the only boat to leave Dover for Calais. He was in high spirits when he took his departure.

(HDM)

Letter From Lady (Marjorie) Nunburnholme

In the present crisis there must be many men and women eager to come forward to be trained and to join attachments. Classes in first aid and nursing have therefore been arranged at the Voluntary Aid Headquarters, Peel House, Spring Bank, where all information may be obtained. P.S. Sewing and invalid cookery classes are in course of formation.

(HDM)

An advertisement offering property for sale in Anlaby Park Garden Suburb included three-bedroom houses at £435 and £415, according to size, and four-bedroom ones at £529 and £550.

(HDM)

What Happened to Wilson Liner
(London, Monday)

With regard to the reported seizure by Germany of two British vessels, the German Embassy states the facts as follows: The Wilson liner *Castro* was in the Kiel Canal and was ordered by the German authorities to proceed to Hamburg for military reasons, as it was not desirable that any commercial vessel should be in the canal at present.

(HDM)

Capture of Supposed Spy on The Humber
Defending Soldier Wounded

Our Grimsby reporter telephones this afternoon that an exciting incident occurred at Waltham near Grimsby this morning, resulting in the capture of an alleged spy, supposed to be a German military officer. Waltham is the Admiralty Wireless Station; it is guarded by a detachment of the 2nd Border Regiment. One of the sentries noticed two men acting in a suspicious manner between the wireless station and the G.N. Railway. They were apparently endeavouring to locate the supply of the current. On being challenged the men ran away. The sentry raising the alarm, the men were chased and one of them succeeded in getting clean away but the other was caught. During the incident one of the soldiers, Private Filbert, of the 2nd Border Regiment, received a bayonet wound in the leg and was taken to Grimsby Hospital. The captured man was brought to Grimsby and lodged at the County Police Station.

[The following day]
Prisoner Discharged Today

Deputy-Chief Constable Osborn stated the prisoner had been observed on three successive days in the vicinity of the wireless station, apparently reading a German book ... His lodgings had been thoroughly searched but nothing of an incriminating nature had been discovered. He was a clerk and had been in the employ of Messrs. Wintringham and Sons, timber merchants, for about twelve months ... Prisoner, a well-dressed man of about thirty years and speaking several languages, was then discharged, the Chairman (Canon Quirk) pointing out the grave danger to anyone loitering near any Government depot at the present time.

(HDM)

A Voice for Peace: 'Now that the papers are full of war, and the inhabitants of the British Isles are asked to show their patriotism, is it not time some move should be set afoot whereby anti-war populace can show their disgust at the unnecessary waste of lives which will inevitably result if we are plunged into European War. Here is a chance for our Social Reformers to come out and show their sincerity. Hoping this will catch the eye of an abler penman than myself.'   (HDM)

(b)
The Home Front
The Zeppelin raid on Hull, 6 June, 1915 — and the aftermath.

Patriotism remained high, though within a few months the mood had become more sombre. The war was not the brief interlude before things returned to normal, as some had tried to hope, and the lists of men and boys — many were in their teens — wounded, killed or missing, became a regular item in the local newspapers and occupied more and more space. This was a cruel war, with the Germans and their allies dug in their trenches, fighting for years over the same stretch of mud.

Those back home soon realised that it was also a new kind of war and that they, too, could face an enemy attack. Zeppelin raids began, and Hull, Beverley, Driffield, Goole, Grimsby, Hedon and Scunthorpe were among the local places undergoing the new and frightening experience of bombs descending from the sky. Many people in the country saw and heard Zeppelins passing overhead and everyone claimed, 'It came just over my house!'

Lighting restrictions were enforced and Hull, which experienced its first — and most serious — raid on 6 June 1915 (see page 42) became known as 'the darkest city in the Kingdom'. The upper parts of street lamps were painted Oxford blue, and the lower parts Cambridge blue. Windows on the upper decks of trams were painted sepia, and curtains covered the windows on the lower decks; two blue lamps lit the gloomy interior. When the dread buzzer sounded, lights had to be extinguished. Fines of 10s 6d or more were imposed for breaches of the regulations and £5 was not uncommon.

There were no air-raid shelters provided by the Government, and the natural tendency was to escape the risk of being buried under the rubble of a house and rush to the outskirts of a town. Hull people in the west of the city often made for Pickering Park, and in the east Mr. T. R. Ferens opened up his stables as a refuge. A post-war, retrospective account of the air raids stated: 'To tell of people taking cover under rhubarb leaves, of portly ladies lying in dykes, of men hiding, of those who donned their Sunday clothes, taking their trinkets, or "trekking" with their household goods, with cats, dogs, canaries and parrots under their arms, are too commonplace, though one good lady certainly deserves "mentioning in despatches", for she was hurrying along with a large ham grasped in both arms!' Under the stairs was considered the safest place by those who took heed of the official encouragement to stay indoors.

Lack of knowledge intensified fear, and even sensible people had exaggerated ideas of what could be heard and seen by the men in the Zeppelin looming overhead. Parents sometimes told their children to be quiet or speak in whispers in case they were overheard and attracted a bomb, and a serious suggestion was that clocks should be stopped during an air raid to avoid their ticking giving a signal to the enemy. War has its less serious moments. In Hedon, an old man living in an alms house in Burgess Square is said to have accepted responsibility for the destruction of the nearby Primitive Methodist Chapel. A bomb fell just as he put a lighted candle on the front doorstep to tie his bootlaces. 'Well, I've nobody but myself to blame,' he said. In a raid on Scunthorpe a bomb fell, unexploded, on the mantelpiece of an 84-year-old woman's home. She threw a bucket of water over it and asked a friendly policeman to 'take the nasty thing away'.

The reporting of raids was prohibited by emergency regulations, and official communiqués merely refer in the vaguest terms to 'a portion of the North East coast'. Rumour flourished under censorship and there are, inevitably, discrepancies in the different accounts which later became available, though these are not fundamental. One apparently authentic report states that the alarm was sounded 48 times in Hull as Zeppelins were spotted approaching the city, and that seven actual raids took place: of course, such statistics depend on how one defines a raid. Another source summarises the total casualties in Hull as 43 killed, 11 died from shock and 115 injured, figures which are not identical with those printed in a popular pictorial summary of the Zeppelin raids on Hull.

Those who experienced the raids have vivid memories of the terrible noise of the engines, the nearness of the enemy, and the way the Zeppelins (with only basic navigational aids) followed roads, rivers, railway lines and the Humber coast, and used such landmarks as a factory chimney in an attempt to locate their target. Those who suffered most in Hull were the poorer people and the casualties included women and children; both facts intensified the horror and the outrage felt.

There is no doubt that Hull people also felt great resentment at the way they had been left undefended when the raids began. As a result of a chance encounter, the novelist, Arnold Bennett, made an entry in his journal about the feeling in Hull. He recorded on 13 December, 1916:

'Lft. R. of a mobile A [nti] Aircraft Unit ... came for tea ...
he said that after big raid at Hull end of last year about,
when Mayor of Hull had been assured that Hull was one of
the most heavily defended places, and a Zeppelin dropped
15 bombs in the town, the population afterwards mobbed
offices, and A.A. Officers coming into the town had to put
on Tommies' clothes. Also that Naval unit was
telegraphed for and that when it came with full authorized

special lights, the population, angry at lights, assaulted it
with stones and bottles and put half of it in hospital, and
had ultimately to be kept off by the military.'
Once defences were installed, the Zeppelins flew higher and one lady,
then a girl in Hornsea, has never forgotten the beauty of a Zeppelin caught
in the beams of searchlights, a sight which held her spellbound and made
her forget all danger. At Hornsea, too, apparently, it was the custom to give
warning of an air raid by lowering the gas supply three times in succession
so that each house with gas lighting had its silent, unmistakeable signal.

Patriotism may not have waned, but it could degenerate into fanaticism,
and a sad chapter in local history was the desire for revenge and the
consequent outbreak of attacks on anyone with a German-sounding name or
with the remotest alleged link with Germany. The sinking of the liner, the
Lusitania, by the Germans, resulted in an instant outbreak of violence
against the innocent. Remarkably, the story from the viewpoint of one
family at the receiving end of the attacks, the Hohenreins, is documented in
considerable detail [see Part Two). An encouraging aspect of the press
reports is that responsible people usually deprecated the violence and the
injustice of these incidents and that, however appalling their impact, they
were perpetrated by only a mindless minority and were promptly dealt with
by the law.

War offered an opportunity for a strange assortment of interlinked,
confused and otherwise submerged emotions to surface. Particularly
distasteful and in urgent need of the new psycho-analysis were the women
who claimed to be performing a patriotic duty in presenting white feathers
to men not in military uniform. The moral blackmail of a young Grimsby
council employee by a public debate on his duty to enlist demonstrated a
more subtle way to pillory an individual.

Everyone was called upon to 'do their bit', but some families felt that their
share of the 'bit' was rather larger than fairness prescribed. The
correspondence columns of newspapers provided an outlet for bitterness
and other strangulated emotions released under the pressure of terrible
events.

Beneath the enormity of a war waged over the entire world, a large area
of life continued, apparently oblivious of the mayhem all around. The
advertisement inserted in the *Hull Daily Mail* by Mrs. Gore, the wife of the
headmaster of Hymers College (see page 23), is a reminder that at least one
desirable villa in Pearson Park retained the comfortable standards of prewar
days.

It was grossly unfair, but also reassuring. The determination not to give
in and to carry on as if nothing has happened is strong. The desire to live in
peace is at least as powerful as any instinct for war.

(*Note — All excerpts are taken from June editions of newspapers except for those
marked October.*)

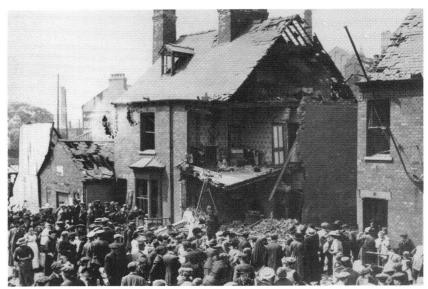

Church Street, Drypool, where a family had a remarkable escape, 6 June 1915.

[G. Michael Kilvington]

Queen Street, Hull, after the Zeppelin raid, 6 June, 1915. [G. Michael Kilvington]

Damage in Waller Street, 6 June, 1915.

Clarence Street after the raid, 6 June, 1915.

Dalton Camp Gala
Relatives and Friends Visit Kitchener's Men
King's Birthday Sports and Fun
[4th June 1915]

Whatever the future may have in store for them, the 12th Service Battalion East Yorkshire Regiment, or the 3rd Hulls as we know them, will not soon forget the King's birthday. The day was given over to pleasure. With military-like precision regimental sports were arranged. The greatest pleasure, though, was from the visits of relatives and friends and the little family reunions which took place. I have motored out to Dalton Holme ... a few times, writes a *Mail* man, but have never seen the camp road so congested. Sandwiched between traps, motor cycles, brakes and transport waggons, it was quite a miniature 'on the road to the Derby', a time when one appreciates a flexible engine. Even infant carriages with their precious occupants were pushed into safety in the grassy sides.

The fine band of the 3rd East Yorkshire from Beverley ... rolled up in style in a char-a-banc. On foot, too, crowds of visitors came from Kiplingcotes Station to the Dalton Holme 'open house', and South Dalton residents, who are becoming quite military, of course, made a call.

The gala day spirit was in the air, yet frivolity was not always the dominant note. Let us direct our gaze towards one corner of the encampment. There is an elderly woman talking quietly, happily and thoughtfully to an only son. Young wives with a child or two forget their anxieties in the reunion with their husbands. At the hedges by the entrance not a few men were expectantly on the look-out for a welcome visitor, whilst some of the jovial spirits teased them with the remark, 'There is no one coming to see you!'

(HDM)

Anti-German Demonstrations
Angry Scenes on Hessle Road
Four Shops Attacked

Anti-German demonstrations took place at Hull on Saturday night. Happily, however, though the scenes were threatening, the damage was not on a large scale. Four shops on the Hessle Road, and one pork butcher's shop in Charles Street, were attacked, and at one or two of the shops, a certain amount of feeling was displayed. There was, however, no looting. The police connected with Gordon Street Police Station, under Supt. Matchan, took steps to quell the Hessle Road demonstrators. One offender was taken into custody and was charged this morning at the Police Court.

A crowd, estimated by the police at from 500 to 600, a large number being women, gathered soon after nine o'clock opposite a shop in Porter Street, where they assumed a threatening attitude. However, the shop was promptly closed, and the demonstrators were persuaded to proceed along the Hessle Road, where in the population is a large element who work at the Fish Dock. The crowd stopped opposite the shop of Mr.Schumm, pork butcher. The shutter had been lowered and the lights were out. Hessle Road on a Saturday night is usually pretty lively and, naturally, the crowd swelled to big proportions as the demonstrators proceeded on their way. At Mr. Schumm's, 180, Hessle Road, windows of the upstairs rooms were smashed.

Women appeared to be the most inflamed among the crowd, and they were certainly the noisiest. Some of their language was strong and threatening. Considerable alarm was felt as the crowd proceeded along the Hessle Road. Mr. Schumm's second shop, where the son is in charge, was visited. Here there is no shutter. The lights were turned out, and the blind lowered. This, however, did not save the shop windows. The large plate glass in the shop was smashed, and then the windows upstairs were attacked. At each smashing of glass there came cheers and jeers from the crowd. Stones, bottles, and bolts were thrown, some of them falling among the crowd. It is stated that a shower of bolts was thrown from the top of a tramcar, and that several of the rioters carried flash lamps. A daughter of Mr. Schumm, very much frightened at the attitude of the crowd, hastened from the shop with the grandchildren. As far as can be ascertained, however, no serious personal injury was happily suffered.

It seems regrettable that naturalised British subjects of the type of Mr. Schumm should be subjected to these attentions. Mr. Schumm has been naturalised now about 40 years. He is widely known in West Hull, and with the family is much respected. He is known not to view with favour the fiendish and inhuman methods of warfare of the Germans.

The crowd attacked also two pork shops of Mr. Steeg, Hessle Road. Like Mr. Schumm, Mr. Steeg is a naturalised British subject. The police showed considerable restraint, and contributed no doubt to preventing of more serious rioting.

(EMN)

A Charles Street Shop

In central Hull some serious disorder occurred in Charles Street, where a pork butcher's shop had the plate-glass windows smashed. The bedroom windows were also smashed, and the crowd threw stones and other missiles. A number of police from the Fire Station dispersed the crowd, who sang in chorus, 'You made me love you, I didn't want to do it.' Another shop in the same vicinity had the windows smashed.

(EMN)

Crowd Attacks Shop
Tradesman's Windows Broken

About midnight a crowd of youths and men were in Waterworks Street, assuming a threatening attitude in front of the premises of Mr. Hohenrein, pork butcher. They were moved on by the police. Later two youths threw a huge stone through the window, smashing the same. The delinquents were pointed out to the police and arrested, the crowd making no attempt at rescue. A Territorial remonstrated with the offenders. The crowds mistook Mr. Hohenrein for a German due to his name. As a matter of fact, the father of the present Mr. Hohenrein was a naturalised Englishman, and Mr. Hohenrein was a member of the East Riding Yeomanry.

(EMN)

Points of View — Letters to the Editor

(i) A correspondent suggests that 'a committee of gentlemen should be got together in Hull to form a corps of aviators and to provide air machines, about 10 in number, for the protection of the city.'

(HDM)

(ii) A correspondent using the pseudonym, 'Curiosity', asks, 'Why is it that in all the Zeppelin raids over England we have not heard of the least damage being done to the life and property of the naturalised alien living in sublime contentment among us. Is it possible they have a secret code of signals indicating where they lie fermenting their hate, or is it that, since we have proved they are in league with the evil one, he insures them as a reward for their cooperation?

Perhaps our airmen may investigate for us, without having to go further to satisfy our curiosity.'

(HDM)

(iii) Suspicious Lights: 'If it is understood that a half brick is to be expected wherever a light is exposed instantly and without warning, it will put a very severe stop to carelessness. I for one would deem it my duty when the order is given for lights out to at once put out any light I see effectively and without notice.'

(HDM)

(iv) Letter From a Mother of Three Soldiers: 'There are a lot of married men who have not any children at all. Why don't they enlist? Never mind about a single man because he doesn't enlist. The single man has his mother to support. I quite agree with single men enlisting but they talk about married men enlisting with large families. Yes, it is their harvest. Their wives have more money now than ever they had in their lives and they don't know how to take care of it; their poor husband at the front and their children running without boots while they go drinking the money. When a married man enlists his wife is well looked after.'

(HDM)

(v) From a Soldier's Daughter, Newbridge Road, Hull: 'When a mother or family is dependent on a single man I should be the last one to think he ought to go, but I am confident there are dozens of single men who have no ties of any sort, and some of the married men have left good positions and families to do their bit for our King and country. One I know of left a position in the city and five children, the eldest only 15 years of age, and my own father left one too, and still we see the "knuts" as they are called, still wandering about the town that either won't enlist or daren't. They are the men that should go.'

(HDM)

(vi) 'Sir, In consequence of the serious state of our country, I would suggest that all people do not go to places of amusement till the war is settled, and that they take care of their money. What was thus saved could be given to the families of those who lose their fathers in defending the cause of England. Also, will all people, good or bad, attend some place of worship on Sunday next.' — 'One Who Has Two Brothers At The War.'

(HDM)

(vii) Blue Tramcar Windows [painted blue to obscure lights and prevent sighting by Zeppelins]: 'Allow me to make some comment about the painting of the windows of the trams. I had the unpleasant experience of riding in one last week ... When I first got into the car I looked at the faces of the passengers, and they just looked as if they had been seasick or recovering from a bad bilious attack.'

(HDM October)

(viii) Skylights at Wartime:'We darken our windows and people are run in for allowing a light to shine across the road. But I have only just realised that Hull houses are very well off for skylights. Here we have been worrying because the shop will not send dark blinds ordered over a week ago, and only last night I realised we cheerfully burn a bright gas on a dark landing which has no windows — and behold it is under the skylight! ... In my one experience of air raids — I won't say in what city — as soon as the excitement began, the houses opposite began to light up — so much so that I sent our soldier servant across to one house to tell them either to shut their door or put out their gas.' — 'Passer By'

(HDM)

'When The Buzzers Blow'
by an East Yorkshire Sergeant

We're stationed in a city
Where the street lamps seldom light,
And there's one eternal question,
'Will the buzzers blow tonight?'
You can hear it at street corners,
You can hear it in the pubs,
And, if things don't very soon alter,
They'll be shouting it from tubs.

(HDM)

Newspaper Prohibition on Publicising
A defence of the prohibition on newspaper reports
of districts bombed

One can imagine that the officers commanding the Zeppelins would look out eagerly for information in the English press. Every district named would be, as it were, a sailing direction for the next raid. The officers might say — to take a purely imaginary case — 'We thought that great dark patch we dropped our first bomb on was a park, but from what the English papers say, it is evident we were entirely mistaken. We shall know better next time.'

If we have a criticism to offer it would be that the authorities would have been wiser to state what the casualties were at the first possible moment. If the officials responsible had heard, as the present writer did on Tuesday, wild fictions about many persons being buried alive in a music hall and so forth, they might have reflected that to prevent the circulation of such stories is easy and is really part of the professed policy of the Government, in the interests of which all the measures of the Press Bureau are exercised.

(HDM)

Alien's Culpable Negligence

A Dane, named Nils Hanson, was charged with failing to notify the police of a change of address. Prisoner is a seaman and was living in Wassand Street and on coming back from sea found that his landlady had moved and did not notify the police that he had also changed his address. He had been warned by the police that he must do so. [Sentenced to 2 calendar months' imprisonment.]

(HDM)

Women Tram Conductors
Innovation in Hull

No women under 25 to be engaged. More conductors than drivers leaving, losing 2 daily.

(HDM)

Wanted for government warwork at Leeds, labourers, 6d. per hour (including 5% allowance for good timekeeping payable monthly). Overtime, time and a quarter. Good chance piecework. Piecework jobs, constant work; no man on Government work need apply.

(HDM October)

Wanted end of October an experienced housemaid — waitress, over 25, 2 in family, late dinner, good holidays. Churchwoman preferred. Apply first instance by letter, stating age, wage and references — Mrs. Gore, North Lynn, Pearson Park, Hull.

(HDM October)

Hull Trades Council
Letter from T.R. Ferens, M.P.

I am afraid, to be quite candid, that there will be little chance, or no chance, of any additional benefit being given in the early future to old age pensions, owing to the terrible cost of the war. The finances of the country must necessarily be greatly strained.

(HDM)

Holderness Hall — Cinema Programme

Sister Susie Sewing Shirts For Soldiers is a comedy drama, founded on the popular pantomine song. *The Lusitania's Last Voyage* gives splendid views of the giant liner in New York Harbour. She is seen casting her moorings and she steams away amidst a scene of great enthusiasm.

(HDM)

Letters Home

To Miss Jessie Wilson of 2 George's Terrace,
Tadman Street, Hull, from Private R. Tucker,
1st/4th East Yorks., 'Somewhere in France':

'We came out here with the intention of doing our bit to keep the old flag flying. We left Newcastle one Saturday and were in the firing line a few days later. It was sharp work for us, and I might tell you it was hard work too. We had a good leader who feared nothing and that was good old Colonel Shaw ... We are not allowed to state where we are but the ruins of fine buildings and the sights we see are shocking.'

(HDM)

From Corporal T. Bonnett,
'Somewhere in France', to his father in Market Rasen:

'Dear Dad,
My pal and I have just finished the tongue between us, so we haven't done very badly, have we? I am real happy today, for just before I started tea our captain came and read to us all a long telegram from Headquarters telling about the tremendous successes we are having all along the line. I think we have up-to-date something like 25,000 prisoners, which is great, don't you think? ... I am just going on duty, so must close and will tell you all when I come home.'

(HDM October)

Our Holderness Letter by 'Paul Pry'

Last Saturday at Withernsea quite a large number of lighting cases came before the justices. Some of the excuses given by the defendants were most trivial, and in some cases it seemed as though there had been gross carelessness. Also it seems there is a disposition to flout and minimise the authority of a special constable in some quarters ... There may be different interpretations of the law and the popular verdict may not be very complimentary, but the fact remains that it is the law and, like the famous Six Hundred, it is ours not to reason why ...,

One of the principal topics of conversation amongst the farmers at Hull corn market on Tuesday was the change in the income tax. Some of them are only just realising what it will cost ...

Some of the vicars and churchwardens who had decided to abandon the evening services in their churches on account of the lighting difficulties have been rather astonished at the volume of opposition to the ideas, and to placate their patrons they are having to make arrangements to obscure the lights so that evening service can be held as usual. It is often a literal impossibility for people engaged amongst cattle to get to church or chapel before the evening.

In the Hatfield and Sigglesthorne districts farmers have adopted to some extent the suggestions made by the Board of Agriculture some time ago with respect to the stacking of corn in the fields, and not all in one place or in the stackyard, so as to minimise as much as possible risk from raiders' incendiaries. Dotted here and there about the fields are pikes and stacks, about a day's threshing in a place, a very wise if inconvenient arrangement.

(HDM October)

Bugler G.H. Gravell of Goole: 'I hope that, whatever may be the consequences, we from Goole may prove a credit to the friends and the town we have left. I am pleased to tell you my wound [in the leg] is going on as well as can be expected, although I cannot get about much as yet without it paining me ...'

(HDM)

A Goole gunner writes from 'Somewhere in France': 'I am still in the pink of health. I received your welcome letter and shall get parcel when I leave the trenches, but when that will be I cannot say.'

(HDM)

Convalescents at Normanby Park

When I approached Normanby Park — the seat of Sir Berkeley G.D. Sheffield, Bart. — on Tuesday afternoon, the sun was shining, and the fine Hall, in the Italian style, standing in its oak-studded Park of nearly 300 acres looked the last place to be associated with war or its attendant horrors. But, truly, war has a way of making people wondrous kind, of making King and peasant, lord and cottager, more to each other than ever before. Were I to devote the whole of my space to the virtues of Lady Sheffield, the veritable Lady Bountiful of Normanby Park, I should then be unable to express all the admirable qualities of this most charming lady. When I arrived I found her in the Red Cross garb which, may I respectfully remark, suits her admirably ... The dining room has been dismantled and made into a sleeping ward for 20. The library and smoking room have undergone the same operation and a start has been made on the drawing room ... An attractive wooden building has been erected in the centre of a flower garden for two patients requiring open air treatment after having been gassed.

(HDM)

Mrs. E. Hall, 6 Marsh Street, Scott Street, Hull, would be grateful for news of her son, Driver B.W. Hall, Transport Section, 4th East Yorkshire Regiment. In his last letter he refers to his regiment coming out of the trenches. It is nine weeks since she last heard of him.

(HDM)

(c)

Peace — 11 November, 1918

Little needs to be added to the newspaper items about the ending of the war. They convey the mixed emotions of relief, joy, exhaustion and sadness which were generally felt after four long, terrible years. There was great excitement, flags were brought out, and the parties spontaneously organised in the streets and terraces of the towns and in the villages are remembered as highlights of their lives by people who were children at the time and were photographed, sitting on forms and grinning at the camera, rather puzzled why normally serious adults were behaving in such an extraordinary way.

The casualties in a war out of control and with a self-perpetuating momentum of attack and counter attack had been on a hideous scale and few families did not suffer directly or indirectly. A generation of young men was devastated and when the next war came there were many elderly spinsters still thinking, rarely talking, of what might have been. Men with an empty sleeve in their jackets, walking on crutches with one trouser leg pinned up, or shaking with paroxysms of coughing as a result of mustard-gas attacks regarded themselves as lucky, probably amazed, to be alive. Those who returned 'shell-shocked' may have preferred death to the nightmare existence which was now their destiny. The formation of 'pals', units of men from the same town who enlisted together and served with friends and relations was intended to encourage, and benefit from, comradeship, but the consequence in a war which regarded men as cannon-fodder was the inevitable wiping out of virtually all the young men in a family or a street. All war memorials are a silent but powerful commentary on past events, but the most pathetic are the smaller ones, sometimes just a tablet on a wall, with a bleak recurrent litany of identical surnames.

The war was over, but one of the newspaper reports hints unsuspectingly at a new and deadly enemy still to be faced. An influenza epidemic spread through Europe and killed more people than the war itself. It was a cruel epilogue to a cruel chapter of history.

Lights on Armistice Day

Now that [the] armistice is confidently expected to be signed, the question of the lighting restrictions will come to the fore. A Hull merchant under the name of 'Lights Up' has sent a letter to the *Mail* suggesting that lighting restrictions being relaxed on peace day. Why not go one nearer and make it the armistice day? 'Lights Up' says, without increasing the consumption of gas, we should have more light by throwing up the shop blinds, and that the street lamps should be cleaned by any person who could provide a ladder for the purpose, and that the buzzers should blow one long blast.

(HDM)

Demobilisation Difficulties

'Sir, When the time comes for demobilising the forces it should be recognised that a prior claim is held by those men who enlisted in the year 1914. The men who joined the colours in those critical days have borne the brunt of the hardships of the war in many respects. They left good situations which in many cases they will not be able to return to, and many will of necessity have to look to new fields of labour for a livelihood.'

(HDM)

The Armistice
Reception of the News in Beverley

The Mayor of Beverley (Alderman Harry Wray) received the official news of the armistice at the Borough Police Court on Monday last about 11 o'clock, just after he had acknowledged the greetings of his fellow magistrates on his re-election as Chief Magistrate. His Worship at once took steps to make the welcome news known, and quickly flags were floating from the towers of the churches and on public buildings — a signal for a free display of bunting from business premises and private houses. Later on merry peals were rung on the bells of both the Minster and St. Mary's. The shipyard closed down until Thursday, and the various munition works closed for the remainder of the day. The schools which were not already closed for the influenza epidemic were given a half holiday. The streets were thronged with people during the afternoon and evening, and there were intermittent displays of fireworks on the part of individuals. People generally, however, conducted themselves with much restraint. They recognised that, while the occasion was one of gladness, it was not a time for rejoicing, few families in the town having escaped the sorrow of bereavement created by the terrible conflict of the past four years.

(BG)

The Cessation of Hostilities
Service of Thanksgiving in Beverley Minster

The special service of thanksgiving for the signing of the Armstice held in Beverley Minster on Thursday evening attracted a very large congregation.

The Mayor (wearing his robe and gold chain) and Corporation marched in procession from the Guildhall ...

At the close of the service the Band of the 2nd East Yorks, which had accompanied the hymns, played the National Anthems of the Allies, concluding with the military march, *Pomp and Circumstance*. The offertory, which was in aid of St. Dunstan's Home for Blinded Soldiers, amounted to £37.

Canon Nolloth preached from the words: 'The Lord hath done great things for us, whereof we are glad.'

(BG)

Hull in Gay Spirits
Mrs Smiffins and the News
[A humorous column]

What I envy amongst the poor and them that haven't had much schooling is the amount of fun they get out of next to nothing. I'm jealous of the way they can manufacture happiness. People with brains or a lot of money more often than not feel like yawning in each other's company, but give a fisherman or a soldier or a docker or a navvy a tin whistle or a cracker with a paper cap in it and they're amused for hours. When I saw in the City Square six girls, each with one hand on the other's shoulder doing the cakewalk, the first girl ringing a bell and the others singing a jumble of nonsense, I said to myself, I did, 'Sarah, look at life. Here's three girls as happy as larks on a summer morning, forgetting there's such a thing as tears, shouting themselves hoarse with delight, and over there is Emperors and Kings as miserable as Satan when somebody he made sure of has got converted.'

(HDM)

Scenes in the Council Chamber

There was an impressive scene in Hull Council Chamber. At 11.45 the Hull Chamber of Commerce assembled for their annual meeting under the presidency of Mr. G.H. Loveridge. The President at the conclusion of his address remarked with some feeling, 'I think it would be a fitting commemoration of the wonderful news that we should sing the National Anthem.' The members filling the Chamber had been waiting for such a sign and promptly everyone rose to his feet and sang, with great heartiness and with feelings of deep thankfulness, the National Anthem.

(HDM)

Wo Ist Der Kaiser?

The shadows are passing — the morning breaks
On a peace that has come to stay,
And the earth from a deadly nightmare wakes
To the dawn of a happier day.

Mary E. Dawe

(BG)

Miss M. Littlewood's Charity Concert

Miss Millie Littlewood, one of the youngest of our teachers of juvenile singers and dancers, gave a very successful performance at the Lyric on Saturday. Miss Littlewood seems to have some justification for the title bestowed upon her of 'the second Annie Croft', for the whole programme was both a compliment to the teacher and the children themselves. As the proceeds will be handed over to the 'Mother Humber Fund' a very acceptable amount should be raised, for the audience was satisfactory.

(HDM)

Holderness Campaign Opens

Captain A. Stanley Wilson M.P. commenced his campaign in Holderness on Friday evening with a crowded meeting in the Council School, Withernsea ... Alluding to the General Election, the speaker said it would be fought under new conditions. At the last election there were in that division 11,000 or 12,000 voters, but now there were 25,000, and 10,000 of those were women, and for the first time all the elections would be held on the same day.

(HDM)

In Memoriam

Haith — In loving memory of Jack, the dearly loved husband of Gertie Haith, killed in action November 13th, 1916.

One of the best

— From his loving wife and little daughter Dorothy.

(BG)

Another view of Edwin Davis's after the raid.

The effect of the raid on High Street, Hull.

Part Two

A FAMILY AT WAR

by

JOHN MARKHAM

This section is based on the Hohenrein Collection in the Local Studies Library, Central Library, Hull, and I gratefully acknowledge the permission given by Humberside Libraries and Arts to make use of the material in this way. I am also grateful to Dr. Charles F. Ross, who donated the collection to the Library on the death of his father, and who has given me every help in the preparation of the manuscript.

For one family the war brought particular pain and anguish. Its members were Hull-born, with fierce pride in their native city. They had prospered in business and were well respected. But when the war came they had one fatal handicap: their surname, Hohenrein, revealed their German origin, and they were to suffer the obsessive cruelty which seems to be reserved for the innocent.

Immigrants were a familiar sight in 19th-century Hull. Thousands of East European Jews fled from the *pogroms*, the violent attacks by their Russian masters, intensified when the assassination of the Tsar Alexander II provided an excuse and an opportunity for greater brutality. In the holds of ships of the Wilson line they braved the hideously uncomfortable voyage from the Baltic ports across the North Sea. Some stayed in Hull; others continued by rail to Leeds or Manchester, and many went on to Liverpool to begin the even longer journey across the Atlantic.

There were also immigrants who came by choice, in a natural desire to find a country which would offer them more scope for the skills they had to offer. The British and German royal families were inter-related and the marriage of Queen Victoria to a German prince brought the two countries even closer together.

Georg Friedrich Hohenrein belonged to this category. He was born in 1832 and it appears that he came to Hull when he was only 16 or so. He worked for a time for a German pork butcher, G. H. Frederick (Friedrich) in Mytongate and in 1850, when he was still only 18, he opened his own pork butcher's shop at 7 Waterworks Street. How such a young man achieved such a feat so quickly in a foreign country remains a mystery and a source of wonder to his descendants. The shop prospered and its reputation grew so high that in later years he merely claimed to be expressing local public opinion when he stated in an advertisement: 'Hohenrein's sausages are the best.' England and Germany combined their might to stock his shop with first quality home-cured ham and bacon, warranted pure lard, celebrated Brunswick sausages and Cassel polonies as well as all kinds of German sausages. On his letter-heads and delivery vans he described himself simply as '*The* Pork Butcher'.

Georg Friedrich married a German girl, Katharine Christine Meyer, who was probably in domestic service and whom he may have met at the German Lutheran Church. A studio photograph shows him as a proud Victorian patriarch standing behind his voluminously skirted wife, a formidable

Georg Friedrich Hohenrein, c.1900.

Mr. and Mrs. G. F. Hohenrein and family,
c.1868.

G. William Hohenrein, the eldest son of
G. F. Hohenrein

G. William Hohenrein, c.1900.

[Humberside Libraries and Arts]

woman with a child on either side. Another, taken c1900, is an impressive portrait of a strong, determined man, bearded and bald, with necktie and high-winged collar, gazing fearlessly at whatever he sees, the master of his own destiny. His ambitions were realised and he opened another shop, No.22 Princes Avenue, a good address in a fashionable area of affluent households. The family home itself was not far away: Derringham Cottage, Derringham Street, at the corner of Victoria Street.

When G. F. Hohenrein died he left a substantial fortune of between £60,000 and £70,000 and the business passed to his eldest son, George William who, very reluctantly, decided in 1907 to leave Hull and settle in Germany because of the poor health of his German wife, Julie — the marriage had been arranged by his father who over-ruled his wish to marry a local girl; his son, usually known as Willy, had been born in Hull. It was a decision with terrible consequences. Abandoning the city and the country he loved was an inconsolable wrench for William. Very like his father, though heavily moustached, he was a man of dignity and strong character, and photographs show him wearing the smart uniform of the East Riding of Yorkshire Imperial Yeomanry with obvious pride. Each year, after his departure, he eagerly anticipated his visit to Hull.

His younger brother, Charles Henry Hohenrein, took over the business and carried on as successfully and confidently as his father. He had been born at Derringham Cottage on 11 May, 1883, educated at the private Eton House School, Albany Street, along with the sons of other Hull parents in comfortable circumstances. When he was 18 he was sent to Germany to study the family trade and two years later he passed the state examinations qualifying him as a master butcher. He was bilingual and fluent in the Swabian dialect. In 1909 he won a gold medal at the Paris International Exhibition, and the Grand Prix and gold medal at a similar exhibition in Vienna. The following year he was similarly honoured in Brussels. He was proud of bringing these distinguished prizes to Hull for no British firm had ever before won them — nor have they since — and they featured with justified pride on his letterheads.

Charles returned to the business in Hull and followed his brother's example by joining the East Riding Yeomanry. He had the strong, open features of other male members of the family and a photograph shows him as a Trooper in the Yeomanry, sitting proudly on his horse. He was a man with excellent prospects and on 25 July, 1911, he married Miss Lilian Agnes Westwood, a local girl who had a fine mezzo-soprano voice and took part in the amateur musical events which were such a feature of the city's lively social life in the Edwardian age. After the ceremony the couple emerged happily from Holy Trinity Church, where friends and family waited to greet them. They had every reason to smile. It was a good time to be alive, especially if you were well-to-do, and Hull was an ideal place in which to begin married life, raise a family and run a thriving business not far away

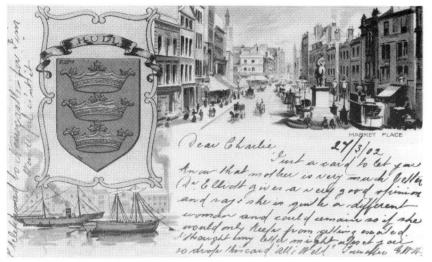

Postcard from G. William to his brother Charles, then in Germany.
[Humberside Libraries and Arts]

Trooper Charles H. Hohenrein, c.1902.
[Humberside Libraries and Arts]

The wedding of Charles Henry Hohenrein
and Lilian Agnes Westwood at
Holy Trinity Church, Hull, 25 July, 1911.
[Humberside Libraries and Arts]

from fine new thoroughfares, Jameson Street and King Edward Street, leading to Queen Victoria Square. These developments had swept away a warren of slums and brought crowds into the city centre to enjoy, or, in the Edwardian expression, to 'patronise', its shops, entertainments and restaurants. A son was born in 1912, and daughters followed in 1914 and 1917.

Charles was paying a visit to brother William in Germany in July, 1914, a time when the crowned heads and statesmen of Europe were frantically despatching telegrams and issuing ultimatums and reminding each other of old alliances. On the station at Coblenz he bought a copy of the *Coblenzer Zeitung*, with a forbidding headline, *'DER KRIEGSZUSTAND ERKLÄRT!'* [War is declared]

Charles managed to get safely back to Hull. In spite of his links with two countries he had no doubt where his loyalty lay and immediately offered to lend his vans to the Government to help the war effort : a letter of reply thanked him for this 'most patriotic' gesture. He volunteered for military service but was declared exempt until 1917, when he was rejected on medical grounds; he then joined the East Riding of Yorkshire Motor Volunteer Corps and served as a sergeant for the remainder of the war. His loyalty, however, counted for little in the frenzied emotional maelstrom which had overwhelmed so many people in that critical and anxious time, and an ominous incident had taken place at the very beginning of the war, for which even a patriotic magistrate found some excuse: 'A regrettable instance of rowdyism in Hull following the declaration of war between England and Germany was afforded by a case heard at the Hull Police Court this morning when Victor Parker and Joseph Connell were jointly charged with breaking a plate glass window in Mr. Hohenrein's shop in Waterworks Street last night and doing damage to the extent of £10... Prisoner [Parker] went into the box and said he was in White-friargate outside the newspaper offices when the declaration of war between England and Germany became known. He was then with his friend and both of them went to the Recruiting Office in Pryme Street, he with the intention of joining the navy and his friend the army... The Magistrate said there was no excuse for the offence he was alleged to have committed, though it might be said that it

7 Waterworks Street, Hull, c.1910.

[Humberside Libraries and Arts]

was done in the excitement of the moment, seeing that the prisoner had just come from reading the declaration of war ... He did not want to prevent him from serving his country if he wished.'

William, left behind in Germany, was in an appalling position : an Englishman in a hostile country. After months of uncertainty, news that he had been sent to an internment camp at Ruhleben came to Hull in a formal greeting on a Masonic Christmas card, bearing the facsimile signatures of the men interned there, among them G. William Hohenrein. Correspondence passed through the Hague, and this arrived before a postcard, written in pencil by William. His son, Willy, a medical student, had been forced to join him there and he used the restricted language of a prisoner which only emphasised the suffering it was meant to conceal:

> 'We are well and as comfortable as circumstances will
> permit. Should be pleased to hear a few more political
> items of family interest to us all. Trusting that you are all
> well. With kind love to you all.'

There were also two Christmas cards, one from the two Hohenreins in Ruhleben camp, bearing an unfulfilled wish for a brighter new year, the other a postcard from Lancaster with a naïve misspelt message, heart-rending in its pathos, from August Schäufler, a German who had been employed in Waterworks Street and who had been interned by the British as an enemy alien. He was joined in his message by a former assistant in Waterworks Street called Kaspar :

> 'We both wish you a happy Christmas as wirk is no dought
> mixed with a lot of trouble. Try to forget them for a time.
> Brightes day will be coming ...'

August Schäufler wrote again on 23 April, 1915 :

> 'Some time ago I received your dear letter. Sorry I was not
> able to write any sooner. We have had a lot of moving
> about in the camp. Thomas with a lot of others were
> transferred to Isle of Man about a month ago. We are not
> allowed to write from one camp to another. Received a
> letter from your brother W., the first one. He says they all
> are keeping fairly well but was troubled a lot about his wife
> ...'

In the early months of the war there were people who tried to believe it would all miraculously blow over, by Christmas everything would be back to normal. It took time for such hopes to die and Charles Hohenrein had had another warning of the clouds gathering when, in November, 1914, he had received a 'comic' but unfunny postcard signed by 'Fritz' with the caption, 'Why don't you come and see us. We're not German' : a crude, anonymous insinuation about his claim to British nationality. Business had continued as normally as possible in Waterworks Street but the imprisonment of William

[Humberside Libraries and Arts]

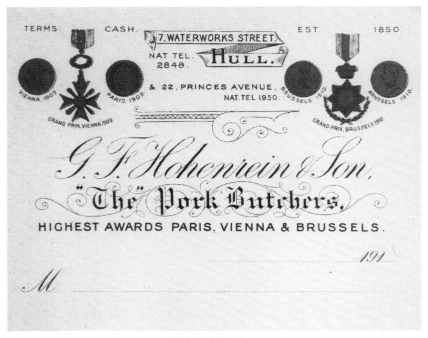

Hohenrein invoice. *[Humberside Libraries and Arts]*

and the internment of staff were deeply felt by a family torn apart by war. Locally, too, a totally unexpected incident had staggered everyone who believed that wars were fought on the Continent and that 'the sanctity of these islands could not be disturbed'.

Farm labourers on their way to work on 16 December, 1914, had noticed great warships off Scarborough, flying the British flag. They had been filled with patriotic pride, though they could not understand why the ships were coming so close to land as if they were making for Scarborough itself. Then the ships opened fire. People in the town assumed it was routine gunnery practice until shells began to smash into buildings. The ships were German, in disguise, and Scarborough was being bombarded.

Some showed their contempt of this unsportsmanlike behaviour of the 'Babykillers Who Flew Our Flag' by ignoring the inconvenient intrusion — like the clergyman who calmly continued his early communion service at St. Martin's Church while the guns boomed outside and who was cited as 'an instance of how Germany's barbarous methods of warfare failed to intimidate Englishmen'.

The bombardment had a different impact on Winifred Holtby, then a boarder at Queen Margaret's School, Scarborough, who was quickly taken with the other girls to a place of safety outside the town. It was her introduction to the horrors of modern war, and international peace was the cause to which she devoted so much of her adult life.

An incident of far greater significance than the bombardment of Scarborough occurred on 7 May, 1915. The Cunard steamship, *Lusitania*, was sunk by a German warship off the coast of Ireland and 1,198 civilian passengers were drowned; to many this was further proof that no deed was too horrific for the barbarous Huns to perpetrate.

The sense of outrage went far beyond rational protest. In war people behave at their worst, as well as their best. Fear and hatred are the enemies of clear thought and fairness, and an innocent scapegoat was as good a target as any other. Xenophobic paranoia spread like a contagious disease and those with German-sounding names were simultaneously accused and found guilty of personal responsibility for the sinking of the *Lusitania*. Mob rule unhesitatingly determined the appropriate punishment. Probably those who enjoyed violence found this an opportunity to their taste.

Hysteria was not confined to Hull. Anyone with a pet dachshund was shunned, some could not bring their lips to utter 'German measles' and invented 'Belgian flush' instead, while John Betjemann was taunted so much about his surname at school that he eventually dropped the final n, which had indicated its apparently Teutonic origin and made the boys dance round him, shouting, 'Betjemann's a spy!'. The Royal Family started to call themselves Windsor, German titles were traded in in exchange for English ones and the Battenbergs became the Mountbattens. For the Hohenreins the sinking of the *Lusitania* was the sound of doom. Their high reputation, their status in Hull society, their loyalty to Britain, the country of their birth, and to their native city were all forgotten. They were now the enemy.

Yet, there was one Hull man who did not forget the past and, at some risk to himself, he sent an anonymous letter of warning on 12 May :

'Dear Sir,
    I belong to a secret gang but I want to be your friend. I wish to warn you that your shop's in danger and perhaps *life* for *God's* sake take this as a warning from one who wishes you no harm (Don't treat this as an Idel Joke) —
                Friendship
I have signed Friendship but I don't know you and you don't know me.'

On a separate sheet he wrote:

'TAKE A GOOD TIP,
DON'T BE ON PREMISES
MAY 13 — 15
OR
MAY 20 — 15'
[A slip probably caused by tension.]

So concerned was the anonymous friend that he wrote a second letter, postmarked the same day, unstamped and costing Charles twopence:

'Dear Sir,
    I hope you got my last letter and I hope you have taken notice of it as your shop is going to be broken up on [blank] and [blank]. I dare not let you know too much as I would be found and I would have to suffer. The reason I have taken such an intrest in warning you is because when I was a boy your parents and those who kept your shop were very good to me many a time when I was hungry and needed bread so you see I wish you no harm in any way. Your shop is not the only shop but there are others and I am warning you and I shall have to carry out my work when I am ordered by my chief the captain. Sir, if you will put a letter in the *Daily Mail* I will know you have got my letter. I do not mean a bold one but one of a mild kind. The reason of it is to av_____

LUSITANIA
Friendship — 2nd'

Throughout Hull there was an orgy of violence, both planned and unplanned, and older people still remember terrible incidents in which the

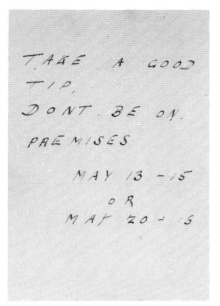

The shop after the change of name,
Christmas 1925. The centre piece is a decorated
boar's head.

The anonymous letter.

Charles Henry Hohenrein at the wheel of his Argyle motor car, c.1914.

[Humberside Libraries and Arts]

homes of kind, respectable people with names of German origin were entered and their furniture thrown into the street.

The attack of which the anonymous letter-writer had warned was reported along with a number of similar cases. It shows that mindless violence received neither universal approval nor the support of the local press:

> 'About midnight a crowd of youths and men were in Waterworks Street, assuming a threatening attitude in front of the premises of Mr. Hohenrein, pork butcher. Later two youths threw a large stone through the window, smashing the same. The delinquents were pointed out to the police and arrested, the crowd making no attempt at rescue. A Territorial remonstrated with the offenders. The crowd mistook Mr. Hohenrein for a German due to his name. As a matter of fact the father of the present Mr. Hohenrein was a naturalised Englishman and Mr. Hohenrein was a member of the East Riding Yeomanry.'

War now reached Hull itself and made the lives of the Hohenrein's a nightmare. Early in 1915, there had been a number of 'buzzer nights' and on 4 June Driffield was the first town in Yorkshire to be raided. Two nights later, on 6 June, came the first — far more serious — raid on Hull.

The buzzer sounded at 10 p.m., public transport was stopped, the lights were dimmed and traffic was given half an hour to leave the streets. At midnight a Zeppelin was spotted approaching Hull from the west. A strange, disturbing feature of the raids was that these were not impersonal attacks from a great height. The Zeppelins had numbers and named captains and, low and purring menacingly, they followed roads and rivers to reach their targets. In the first attack the Luftschiff 9, commanded (it was later discovered) by a renowned pilot, the 'notorious' Kapitan-Leutnant Heinrich Mathy, the most brilliant Zeppelin commander, moved along the Humber coast as far as Marfleet and then made for Hull. No one ever forgot the sight of the airship with its three gondolas 'sailing over the city' at a variety of estimated heights or the sound of its whirring engines and clanging signalling bells. Observers used a variety of familiar images to convey the lasting impression it made on them. To one person it 'appeared not much larger than a cigar', and, understandably, someone on Hessle Road remembered it being 'as large as a big steam trawler'.

East Hull suffered in the raid, with houses destroyed and the occupants killed. The Zeppelin dropped two bombs harmlessly into King George V Dock and then released part of its cargo of high explosives in the area of the old Citadel, on the Drypool side of the River Hull. Timber yards there and Rank's mill escaped, but Hewetson's sawmill and woodyard in Dansom Lane were set on fire. It was the Old Town, however, still a crowded residential area as well as a business centre, which suffered the worst damage. There was a large crater in High Street and Edwin Davis's premises on the south side of Holy Trinity Church were hit: the fire that raged was the fiercest of all those caused by Zeppelin raids. Queen Street was badly damaged, and bombs fell on Princes Dock Side. In the horrifically novel raid 13 high explosives and over 40 incendiary bombs were dropped, 40 were injured, and 25 were killed (if one includes a man in Westmorland Street who fell downstairs and broke his neck in his hurry to leave the house): the fact that all the casualties, who included a number of children, were working class people, roused strong emotions. Great resentment was also felt that Hull was defenceless, and the town's leading citizens urged the War Office never again to leave them so exposed and vulnerable.

The Zeppelin raid must have intensified the Hohenreins' alarm. It seemed now that no horror could be ruled out. The ignorant were determined to retaliate — somehow — and on 7 June, 1915, the local press reported a number of incidents, of which one is typical :

> 'Angry and Excited
> Annie Bates was fined 5s. for being drunk and disorderly
> last night. Evidence was given that the prisoner, who was
> drunk, was trying to provoke a crowd to attack a pork
> butcher's shop.'

Charles Hohenrein felt the need for official support and obtained from the Chief Constables's office a confirmation of his nationality.

> 'The bearer, Mr. C.H. Hohenrein, is a British born
> subject whom I have known since his youth. He is a man
> of the highest integrity and honour, and I have the most
> implicit confidence and reliance in him.
> He is well known to most of the leading citizens in this
> district.'

In a fated attempt to destroy lies by focusing on the facts he offered a substantial sum to anyone who could prove that he and his family were not British by birth:

> 'Owing to the erroneous opinion of the public that we are
> either German or naturalised English, and our consequent
> unpleasant position, we have decided to close until the
> Government intern all aliens, so that we may reopen and
> continue our 65-year-old established business without
> being subjected to unjust threats, insults and much
> inconvenience.
> We are prepared to pay £500 to any local charity if anyone
> can prove we are not English!'

In a circular letter which is a model of English style, infused with the dignity and nobility of an innocent man who is patently far superior to his tormentors, he informed customers:

> 'Owing to the critical period through which we are passing, in consequence of the erroneous opinion of many of the public that we are Germans or naturalised English, we have decided to close until such time as the Government intern all aliens and thus clear the air and show the people that no Germans are at large and that all tradespeople open and trading are either English, as we are, or of a friendly nationality.
>
> It is impossible for anyone possessing a spark of refinement or justice to do business and be subjected to daily insults, base insinuations and threats of which one is innocent by people whose character or morals do not bear investigation.
>
> It is a distressing decision to come to after sixty odd years of unbroken trade, but we feel sure our customers will appreciate our position and rally round us when we re-open, which we hope will be ere long under happier conditions for us all.
>
> We take this opportunity of thanking you for past favours, and trust to enjoy your esteemed patronage again in the near future.'

While her husband and son were imprisoned, Julie wrote to Charles and Lily in German, otherwise the censor would not have allowed it to be despatched. Most of her letters were filled with family and personal matters, messages to, and enquiries about, people in Hull, and the problems of her own poor health, intensified by the separation from William and the loss of her home. 'If only we could all be together,' she wrote on 10 March, 1915. 'When will that happen? Be so kind as to give all our relations and acquaintances our warmest greetings.' There were also financial problems and on 1 April, 1915, Julie expressed her obvious disappointment at receiving a poor rate of exchange on some dividends — amazingly still — received from Hull: 'Could Mr. Pearce not try to send it to a bank in Holland which could send it to the Bavarian Handelsbank, Würzburg, then there would be less expense involved, or send it to the American Consul in Holland who can send it to me ... Oh, if only we had never seen or heard anything of shares.' They lived modestly on William's inheritance and on the money Charles had paid him to acquire his share of the business. A little later in the year, 14 November, she longed for the impossible — 'I need good food, rest, fresh air and, above all, no worries' — but, more practically, asked Charles to 'send some bacon ... perhaps also a tongue in tins, some peppermints' to her husband and son.

The 'great loss' of their money was an added burden. 'We haven't deserved such things to happen to us,' Julie wrote, accurately but uselessly, on 18 February, 1916. 'If only things were still as they were five years ago. The dear Lord alone knows what will become of us. I hope we never end up in Lister's Homes [in Hull]!' Then, in a period when the mundane carried great significance, she continued by asking 'dear Charlie' to send a piece of bacon or salted chine or ham to the prison camp, 'at our expense of course'.

A letter from William, dated 21 July, 1915, in what Charles must always have regarded as the darkest period of his life was significant for more than the news it brought from Germany. It was addressed to C.H. Hohenrein, but 'Ross' had been written over 'Hohenrein'. The German surname had become an intolerable burden and Charles had been driven to destroy this link with the past. He had a good friend named Ross: it was short and easy to pronounce both in English and German and, in fact, it is not unknown as a German surname.

William's letter is one of great literary quality with its dignified and moving expression of the family's tragic circumstances, and their total bewilderment and inability to comprehend the cruelty inflicted on them:

'Dear Charlie and Lily,

We were, as you may well imagine, very happy indeed to hear that you are alive and well. It would be impossible for me to describe the suspense and the agony of mind we were all in until your letter arrived to reassure us, and our earnest prayer is that Heaven may preserve you all from any calamity and similar visitations ... How your last words on the departure platform at Würzburg last July are still echoing in my ears. "I wish you were coming with us." Yes, how much suffering and misfortune could have been avoided, how could I not have exercised my usefulness in many other respects instead of leading a useless life now for nearly nine months as a British prisoner of war at Ruhleben. Here we are, three of us, Fred [a nephew, the eldest son of his brother, George], Julie and myself cut off from all we hold most dear, and filled with thoughts of those in dear old Hull, whose memory we cherish and whom we all so reluctantly left behind. I can assure you that if I had had the remotest idea of war breaking out between England and Germany I should certainly have come along with you. As you are all well aware, it was only for reasons of Julie's health and repeated medical advice that we ever left Hull. To me it was a great sacrifice. The severing of the friendly intercourse of old associations to reside in a country which is quite strange, whose customs are different, and where everything with which one is surrounded is so inexpressibly foreign to one's ideas is a matter better imagined than described. This must have manifested itself to you by my annual visits to Hull, the city of my nativity, which always did me good — to which I hope to return as soon as I once again regain my liberty. There seems to be quite a number of prisoners interned here who complain that, on account of their possessing German names, their wives and children in England have been subject to violence and outrages. This I cannot believe, this is entirely un-English and until I have more definite news upon the subject shall very much doubt its accuracy. Besides what is a name? Merely a legacy inherited from our ancestors and in our case one of which we may be justly proud. But at any rate this would be impossible to happen to us. Our services in the interests of the British public will not be easily forgotten and our loyal sentiments no one can doubt.'

Charles (Hohenrein) Ross's son, Dr. Charles F. Ross, has some interesting recollections of life on the inside during this period:

'I was 6 when the war ended, so I do have a few memories of it, such as being awoken during the night and taken down to the underground air raid shelter which my father had had built in the garden of Derringham Cottage, Derringham Street, Hull, where the family was living. This shelter, known to us as the "dugout", was of substantial construction and held about 10 people on comfortable benches and was heated by a solid fuel stove. The only snag was that it was below the water table and had to be kept free from flooding by means of a hand pump in a sump. Sandbags protected the thick concrete roof and we all felt quite safe in it. I can remember seeing a Zeppelin in the searchlights and AA shells bursting well below it on one occasion. Certain stupid persons spread a rumour that the weather vane on the roof of the house was a direction indicator to the airships! I well remember the "buzzers" which I believe sounded from the now demolished Blundell's works on Beverley Road corner. My father was a friend of the then Chief Constable and had prior warning of impending air raids from him over the telephone, the code being "Please deliver the usual order of sausages"!'

Only one side of the correspondence is available — the letters from

Eton House School, Albany Street, Hull, c.1921-2. The Principal, James Simpson's class.
Charles F. Ross is third from left on the second row from the front.

[Humberside Libraries and Arts]

Germany — but some indication of the indignities suffered by the Hull branch of the family must eventually have reached William. In an official postcard from Ruhleben he wrote as Prisoner No. 11 from Baracke No. 7 on 27 April, 1916, his flowing style constrained by the allotted space:

> 'My dear ones, Many heartfelt thanks. Parcel of margarine Mar 22 to hand. Others probably lost. 14 days without butter. Godsend. Julie and Else middling. Cannot obtain necessaries. Hard times. Is Pearce sending monthly allowance? Poor Fred Allan. My heart aches. Am in constant anxiety for you all. You cannot conceive. Please also send black wool for repairing stockings. May God help us all.'

This was followed by a letter of 10 August, 1916, from his home in Würzburg. He had been released 'on leave until further orders' though his son was still detained. He was filled with brotherly compassion for the plight of the Hull family, which was as bad as internment:

> 'Without speaking of any physical pains, the mental anguish has been terrible. We ourselves are powerless to

do anything and can only rely upon the help of the Almighty in whom alone we can place our trust...'

His wife, Julie, whose health had improved a little since the release of her husband added at the end:

'My dear Willy came home on 26th July, the anniversary of mother's death. He has changed very much and his beard made him look very old and worn. You will both imagine how I felt after 21 months departure. If only I were better in health. I am far from well but I did feel a little better when Willy came home.'

Another fine letter, written on 13 September, 1916, in William's dignified style of which he was such a master, conveyed the anguish, not merely of the family but of all the people in similar situations:

'We are all in great suspense and anxiety as to your welfare. Like yourself I have much to relate when we meet again. Please God, it may be soon. If our prayers, hopes and wishes could bring about an early and abiding peace, I am sure we should not have to wait long ... For some reason I would rather that Willy [his son] had been released. So much time is being wasted and the years that are fast slipping by are going without any progress being made.'

The affection with which August Schäufler, the German employee, regarded the family warmed his simple letters, which were scrutinised by a censor before they could be sent on to Hull. 'I am sorry your dear wife suffers so much with her nerves,' he wrote on 15 September, 1916. 'No doubt the time we are living in is enough to try and shatter anybody's constitution.'

Once the insane outburst of revenge and hatred following the sinking of the *Lusitania* and the Zeppelin raids had spent itself, Charles Ross had resumed business on 3 November, 1915, no doubt to the relief of his customers, some of whom had cause for shame. In war there is a natural desire to maintain whatever links with normality may be salvaged from the chaos all around. A steady flow of orders eventually reached Charles Ross from Hull people who had been interned and longed for a taste of the familiar food. August Schäufler acted as middle-man and so continued to serve Hohenrein customers and to maintain a fragile link with the old days; his letters show how the apparently trivial can communicate tragedy as much as great events. He wrote on 6 October, 1916:

'I do not get any news from Hull now. The only sign sometimes is wen someone gets things sent out of your shop. Then I can see by the paperbag that you are still

*'Established 100 years' — Charles H. Ross
outside the shop, 1950.*

Charles H. Ross was a well-known shot.

7 Waterworks Street, Hull, after bombing in the Second World War.

alive. Keep the shop going. I suppose you have heard from your brother Will and that Willy is at home also for the present. I am pleased that he has got out of his misery ... Mr. Ross, would it be too much trouble if I ask you to send me some smokd bacon as befor, fairly lean. There is a few old costumers who always bother me. Please put the postage as well on my acct ...'

In a later one he wrote:

'Will you send the following order on Thursday or Friday Xmas week. 6lb loin, pork pie about 3lb, about 3lbs lean smoked bacon ... then make up the money with a few Frankfurt saus or Wiener. Send to Mrs. Baumgustel, 129 Welbeck Street. Her husband is with me in the same hut.'

A friend of the family, Frank Baker, now in the army, also longed for the happy times before the war.

'Who knows,' he wrote on 20 September, 'some time in the dim future we may all meet at your place and have one of those special evenings you used to treat us to in the old days ... I can't say I am ill but am sorry to say that I don't feel near as fit as I did last time I came out. Perhaps it can only be expected as you know that I was wounded. Can't stand the weight of my pack *etc*. as I used to. A little extra exertion and I am reminded that my internal organs are not near as strong as they might be, but with a bit of luck no doubt I shall go through alright.'

On the envelope Charles Ross in old age added a brief but terrible note on the tragic fate of Frank Baker: 'He was wounded again in the spine and operated on 14 times but after 17 years in bed died.'

The war finally dragged to an end and the Waterworks Street shop recovered from the nightmare and was serving the people of Hull and district with its excellent products, as if normality had never been interrupted. 'Chas. H. Ross' was now the name above the shop, but people often referred to it as 'Hohenrein's'. It suffered again in the Second World War, having to be substantially repaired after the Blitz, and business continued until 1946 when Charles Ross retired. It was sold on his retirement, but the name remained. In 1953 it was demolished so that the large neo-Georgian Queen's House could be built on the site of bombed and ageing property. Waterworks Street was incorporated in Paragon Street and its name disappeared.

War did not end the sufferings of the Hohenreins in Germany. It was a time of great hardship and financial instability and William's letters made it sadly clear that peace was not the idyllic life for which they had hoped and prayed. Even before the end of the war he had been repatriated and in January, 1918, was in Hull. In a newspaper interview he described the atrocious conditions at Ruhleben; he had shared his bed with a cousin of General Smuts and formed a friendship which seemed likely to last. During 1917 his wife, Julie, was seriously ill and his daughter, Else, was recovering from a major operation, and he had been allowed to visit them at Würzburg. If the newspaper report is correct, he must have been recalled to the camp after the earlier grant of permission to leave until further orders. He died in 1933.

Charles Ross, living in the old family home in Derringham Cottage, became an important man in many aspects of the city's business and social life. He was a director of Hull City and Suburban Cinemas which built the Regal [now Cannon] Cinema in the newly opened Ferensway in 1935 and this was followed by others of equally grand name, the Rex, the Royalty and the Regis in Hull, and another Regal in Beverley. He was chairman and managing director of Hull Palais de Danse on Anlaby Road, which later became a roller-skating rink and was finally destroyed by fire. Always keen on sport, he was a director of Hull City A.F.C. and president of Hull Bowling Club, and regularly went shooting in Holderness, where his prowess as a first-class shot was well known. He spent his 80th birthday shooting wild boar in southern Germany. A freemason and a Rotarian, he made a full contribution to life in the area and he bore no grudge against his fellow-citizens for the appalling way he had been treated.

He remained, like his father, a staunch supporter of the German Lutheran Church in Hull, although after the First World War he did not attend services. He did, however, pray each day in the way he had been taught as a child.

Germany suffered mounting economic crises, and in this context of hyperinflation and despair Hitler and the Nazis came to power. By a supreme irony, Charles Ross's nephew, Willy, who had been interned as an alien in Ruhleben but who later took German nationality, was killed towards the end of the war during an Allied raid on Heilbronn, where he was on duty as a doctor.

In 1946, Charles Ross retired to a pleasant country house, The Paddocks, at Burton Pidsea in Holderness, moving to Cottingham in 1970. His wife had died in 1956 and he was now suffering the failing sight of extreme age. He took great pleasure in the talking books of the Royal National Institute for the Blind, and a neighbour remembers him as a kind and cheerful old gentleman whose spirit only dimmed after the death of his dog. Charles Ross died on 23 August, 1974, aged 91. A detailed obituary of his long and active life appeared a year later in the 'In Memoriam' column of the *Hull Daily Mail* as his family felt that his passing had gone unnoticed. They added a moving postscript: 'This notice is inserted by his children as a tribute to his memory and as a record of service by one who regarded himself as a true Yorkshireman. He was indeed a worthy son of his native city.'

The events of the First World War occurred many years ago but Charles Ross's longevity links them with modern times. History is not irrelevant and it is important that the story of the Hohenreins is not forgotten.

Postscript:—

After the Second World War William Jackson and Son bought the old family house in Derringham Street and subsequently demolished it.

Else, the daughter of G. William and Julie Hohenrein, married Alf Bartelmeh and went to live in the U.S.A. Their only child, an actress who used the name Jean Bartel, became Miss America in 1943.

Fred, the nephew of William and Charles, who was interned with his uncle and cousin in Ruhleben camp, is still alive at the age of 92 and lives in Chiswick. His father changed the Hohenrein surname to Blake. Mr. Fred Blake has a remarkable memory and has been of great help in the preparation of this history.

The Paddocks, Burton Pidsea.   [Humberside Libraries and Arts]

Part Three

REMEMBERING

Local People Remember the First World War

A LETTER FROM DAISY ROBINSON, DATED 14 JUNE, 1915, OF 62 BELVOIR STREET, HULL, TO MRS. STOW: *[This letter is in the Local Studies Library, Central Library, Hull, and has been reproduced by kind permission of Humberside Libraries and Arts. Efforts to trace the writer or any descendants have failed.]*

We are very glad to have got over our experiences of last week — we have now been able to get the arrears of sleep made up — the first few nights of last week being rather unsettled ones: The 'raid' took place on Sunday night — (a week yesterday) — it is difficult, even yet, to get any authentic details as everything has been so much suppressed. At first the deaths were put down at 50 — and the injured persons numbered about twice that (chiefly cases of burning I think). I think though that the total casualties are about 25 to 30 — so far as they know. The bombs fell chiefly in the densely populated parts (near the big works — Ranks, Reckitt's *etc.*). In some cases a full row of terrace houses were demolished. I went myself afterwards to see some of the damage — just the shells of the houses left and the poor souls in the neighbouring houses sitting about with perhaps all the windows broken in their own houses — the roof broken in or big holes in the roadway and the walls. It was a pitiable sight. This district we live in was not

102, Great Thornton Street. In this room five boys were sleeping. Two were stuck but escaped. the bomb penetrated the floor and fell on the bed occupied by Mrs. Needler, who was seriously burned.

damaged, though we had the Zeppelin over the neighbourhood and the engines sounded terribly loud. The nearest bomb fell about ½ a mile away. They were aiming, of course, at the big works — oil-tar, stations *etc.* and came pretty near most of these targets and if it had not been so still a night the fires would have spread. There were big fires and several lesser ones — the sky was lighted up in a huge flare. We have been very lucky in our friends and were fetched out of the house the first time (but not till it was over) and the night of the second alarm (Tuesday) we spent in another friend's garden. I must not weary you with more detail though, as I am sure you will have had enough by now!

MY MEMORIES OF THE FIRST WORLD WAR BY LEONARD M WRIGHT *[Mr. Wright of Waltham, near Grimsby, was awarded a certificate of merit for this essay which he entered in a competition in 1967. He died a year ago and his widow, Mrs. Wright, has very kindly given permission for it to be reproduced.]*

For me the year 1914 was a memorable one. I left the village school and commenced work in my father's wheelwright's shop. Therefore any memories which I have retained will be youthful ones. I was fourteen.

There had of course been rumours of war in the air for a long time, especially in the shape of a German invasion. We youngsters used to get excited and let our imagination run wild at the prospect of an enemy submarine coming up the Louth-Tetney Canal, which was at that time still navigable for barges and small steamers. The fear must have been real, the invasion route a figment of our young minds.

The actual news that hostilities had commenced came in the daily paper (which was then delivered direct by post; we had two postal deliveries by bicycle in those remote days) and this brought almost a sense of relief, even hilarity, after a long period of suspense. Of course everybody 'knew' that it wouldn't last long, with all those 'modern' weapons, even aeroplanes which could carry up to two 20-lb bombs — which were hung over the side of the fuselage; the method of dropping was to cut the tether. Of course these were just illusions.

The early recruiting meetings are well remembered and there was a surge of patriotism from most quarters. Many local lads volunteered at meetings often held in village schools, and the Lincolnshire Yeomanry swelled its ranks. Later, when being transported overseas, their troopship, the *Mercia,* was shelled. Some of the lads are still well known to me.

Many troops were stationed in the area and we had never seen so many men or bicycles down the village lanes before. I remember the swish of the many tyres on the muddy roads. The officers had motor-cycles and to get near one of these machines was a thrill.

One autumn evening, an officer on his Douglas halted where a group of village lads under military age were gathered by the saw-pit. In his perfect southern twang he enquired the way to Covenham St. Mary's, remarking that he had asked several other people but nobody seemed to know of it. One of the lads — he later joined up and drove a traction engine in France — was able to enlighten him with — 'It's up theere. Yah shud a sed Coanum.'

Later came the East Yorkshires, the Suffolks, again cyclists, and then cavalry — the Scottish Horse. It is natural that the latter are best remembered, for one of the sergeants frequently visited our home during which time he taught me to play draughts — and courted my sister. Later, as a commissioned officer, he became my brother-in-law — a true patriot and a grand fellow. Now an octogenarian and alas a widower.

Of the actual crunch of the war, some things quickly spring to mind, though not in chronological order: The Zeppelin raid on Cleethorpes in which those lads from Manchester suffered and died — and I — in my youthful, morbid curiosity — cycled over the next day 'just to have a look'. The resulting exit of Grimbarians to the outlying villages, and the group of cottages at Covenham earning the name of 'Zeppelin Row'.

At home, the fear of invasion prompted the authorities to prepare for evacuation from the coastal areas. Parish meetings were called and at Alvingham it was decided to convert farm waggons and drays into covered waggons for the conveyance of women and children, the men to go on foot, droving the cattle inland as far as Market Rasen, there to await further instructions. The convoy — or was it 'assemblage' — was to be preceded by a cyclist, duly appointed.

The 'covered waggon' arrangements brought extra work to my father and me. We fixed iron hoops, made by the village blacksmith, to the various vehicles, some of which my father had built years before, and these would have been covered with various waterproof sheets in case of need. Fortunately this did not arise.

A memorable day occurred, I think, in the autumn of 1916, when an aeroplane landed in a stubble field at High Field Farm, North Cockerington. Of course I downed tools at once, mounted my newly acquired second-hand cycle and was first on the scene, happy to be able to assist the pilot, a Sub-Lieut. R.N.A.S., to trace his position on the map and direct him to the nearest telephone — at Louth, four miles away. Imagine my surprise and the thrill when he asked me to guard his machine while he went to contact his home station, leaving me wearing his flying coat, complete with revolver, which was probably the only armament of that machine.

The name of that pilot remained with me for years, but has, alas, now faded from memory. I had an additional thrill some time after that incident when I read in the *War Illustrated* that this, 'my' airman, and probably 'my' plane, had made a successful raid on a Zeppelin shed at Dusseldorf, for which the pilot had been decorated.

An incident I still find amusing happened when a British airship came slowly over the village, flying very low indeed, much to our delight. This is best described in the words of the farmer's wife at Manor Farm, when I went to fetch the milk next morning — 'Did ya see that theere greeat thing come ower yisterdaya, it had a greeat roaape traailin and it was ivver sa law, slap atween our pantry an the petty.'

Asul nivver furgitit mesen slong asalive!

The canal, mentioned earlier, was to figure in our minds again, and strengthen our fears of invasion, for troops arrived to prepare the wooded swing bridges for demolition. Some of the soldiers came to our workshop to borrow a cold chisel, which my father willingly lent, with instructions to take care of it and return it later. Eventually the same lads came back, looking sorry for themselves, and haltingly confessed that they had lost the chisel — well, not lost, for they knew where it was — at the bottom of the canal, which was then fairly deep. No doubt it is still there in the mud and silt, but I haven't time to go and look for it now, being busily retired.

There is a sequel to the above incident: in connection with the preparation for blowing up this particular bridge, the explosives were stored in the granary at Lock Farm. On a routine inspection a young officer supposedly struck a match, and found the materials in good combustible condition ... The resultant fire burned the roof and the floor of the granary and severely damaged the blue spindle-sided waggon below. I remember especially the waggon, for my father and I had the task of dismantling and repairing it: no machinery, just hand tools — it called for patience and my father's know-how. The total cost of the extensive repairs and painting amounted to £16-15-0. Our labour was charged at sixpence per man hour.

As the war progressed, labour on the farms became scarce and my father released me from the wheelwright's bench to go threshing. Being an active youth I was given the task of 'band cutting'. Did I say 'task'? Oh, the agony of the first few days. Back ache, hands chapped and scratched, thistle pricks in fingers and if ever there was a constant job it was 'band cutting'. Robert, the threshing machine owner, was a jovial though waspish man, smallish, 'wick as an eel' and a glutton for work. His arms were always open, waiting for the next sheaf. But he was patient with me in my clumsiness and inexperience. I eventually got the knack and rhythm of the job and was able to 'save the bands' — a mark of efficiency. The work became less painful though just as constant. The pay was excellent at five shillings per day.

Food rationing? Not many recollections except that the flour was poor, as was the colour, texture and flavour of the bread. Even the 'kissing crusts' on mother's bread was lacking its usual nutty flavour. Sugar was very scarce, coarse and brown. I remember Harry, the machineman's mate, asking someone to pass the 'sand'. Strange as it may seem, it was during the war while I was threshing, and having my meals at the farmer's table at Poplar Farm that I first tasted apple pie with cheese — and liked it, especially with fresh cream on it.

MRS. A. M. KIRBY, *[aged 92, of Cottingham, in a conversation with her son, Martyn, in July 1988.]*

I was born in 1896 so I was 18 just 8 days after the War started on 4 August. We lived at Tollerton, just outside York, and Mother was the landlady at the Station Hotel. This was only yards from the main railway line between London and Edinburgh. The line was fairly quiet during the war because there were fewer main line trains so that troop trains could travel easily.

There were no ration books and the villagers grew plenty of food in gardens and orchards and shared it round the village. I remember turnips being very common. There were pigs and chickens, and farmers supplied butter to the local shop. This was Mrs. Hodgson's bread shop and I went to work there, having just left Easingwold Grammar School. My sister and I had plans to take over the shop at this time. Things from abroad such as tea, sugar and fruit were in short supply and I had to carefully weigh small amounts into little paper bags so everyone could have some. In general we did not notice any great shortages of food, and flour was ground in three mills. Farmers drove a waggon of corn to the mill, left it and later collected the bags of flour.

Living in a public house was interesting because it was a centre for news, and telephone messages came into the station signal cabin. The farmers put their goods onto the train for York market and left their horses and traps in our stables for the day. Spirits and beer were sometimes limited because there were fewer deliveries and Mother had to close down on some days. She sometimes served tea or coffee with cheese and biscuits when beer ran out. The doctor lived in Tollerton and served several local villages. He had no nurse, and any sick people were taken by trap into the York Hospital. He made his own medicines and believed in giving spirits to patients. There were few drugs like today and he used to send medicine bottles to be filled with whisky and brandy.

Our most exciting war event was to be bombed by a Zeppelin! It must have been following the main railway line northwards. We came out to see it. It was grey and we could hear the roar of its engines and see the Germans in the cockpit. It must have tried to bomb the line or the station but it missed and a bomb exploded in the small wood down the lane that ran past our garden and back field. We used to collect dry kindling from the wood every day and the family had carved their initials on the trees. The bomb burnt down a part of the wood. The village people were scared and one woman collected her best silver spoons and left her sick husband in bed to look after himself as she ran down the road. My youngest sister ran upstairs to count the money in her piggy bank!

There were German prisoners in a camp nearby and they worked the land. Once, a troop of 12 prisoners and 2 guards came by and Mother gave them food. After the war one German wrote a letter to her, thanking her for her kindness.

One of our jobs was to send parcels to the soldiers. I bought khaki wool at 3½d. per ounce and knitted scarves, socks, mittens and balaclava helmets. We sent soap and other goods that would not go bad in the parcel, which was stitched into an unbleached calico cover with big labels painted on the side.

I suppose village life went on almost as normal. It was quiet and simple but people really helped each other.

Interviews with local people

Some of the material which follows is taken from interviews carried out by students from Humberside College of Higher Education as part of their Diploma of Higher Education course, during 1980-83, and some from a programme of interviews jointly sponsored by the College and the Manpower Services Commission in 1984-5 under the title 'Voices from the Great War'. This material is Crown copyright and is published by permission of Her Majesty's Stationery Office. The bulk of the interviews collected in this scheme, which concerned the military and naval aspects of the First World War, is to be published separately.

I should like to thank the M.S.C. workers, Janet Harrison, Tim Nicholl, Maureen Fagan and Lawrence Showler (technician), for their contributions, as well as those people who willingly gave their time to be interviewed. The clarity and vividness of their recollections have given us valuable personal insights into the traumatic years of 1914-1918, and have created a small but unique regional archive of tape-recordings for further study. It is worth explaining that the scheme's brief was to interview people living in Humberside in 1984-5, although they may have been elsewhere during the 1914-1918 period.

Thanks are also due to B.B.C. Radio Humberside for permission to transcribe parts of their Waggoners' Reserve Archive programme.

In some cases no personal details of interviewees are available for publication but otherwise reference is made to contributors' origins and whereabouts at the time of interview.

Peter Adamson.
Former Senior Lecturer in History,
Humberside College of Higher Education.

MR LATHAM *[born Worthing Street, Hull. He and his wife are still happily with us and living in Hull. They were interviewed by Jeanette Rollerson and Ann Paulls in 1982.]*

The houses in Portobello Street during the war were really quite posh. The majority of them were of the yellow bricks, and they still look as good to this day. It would be 1909 when mother took us down there to Portobello Street from Worthing Street off Clough Road, and it was a new house. I lived at No. 87 Portobello Street and it was quite near there that a Zeppelin dropped three bombs. The first one was just behind what is now Rovers' ground. Two young men from two doors away were lying on the bank of a pond when they dropped the second bomb smack right in it. Well, they were O.K., but what a mess! The next one was dropped much further away. We wondered whether they were trying to get a searchlight which was in the allotments at the bottom end of Portobello Street, manned by soldiers. Incidentally, two of those soldiers were sleeping in our house and this night I slept through it all, my brother as well. Next morning these soldiers carried us down and through it all — glass all over, windows gone, what a mess it was! But we slept through it, never heard a thing. That was the worst of it as far as we knew. There was nothing else near to us after that.

When the buzzers went at night the two soldiers used to run up the street, often with us small ones on their backs, to put the street lamps out — they were all gas lamps then. I presume that was done all over Hull, because nobody official came to do them. We couldn't put the lamps on again, so, if it was an early warning they had to stay black all night. That part was quite amusing for us.

At that time, Portobello Street was about the last built-up street off

Holderness Road; behind us were open fields. There were cows and horses in the fields behind us. The field where the pond was, was right on the edge of Craven Street School playing field. All the rest were allotments. There were probably about 200 allotments. A lot of people used to come trooping down to the allotments to get away from the buildings when the buzzers blew. Of course, it was a good tramp down Portobello Street at that time. But it didn't seem to happen for long. Well I suppose they plucked up courage and stayed in and didn't bother to come out after a bit.

We didn't see a lot of the soldiers. We were at school and they were on duty most nights. But we did see them that morning when they carried us two down after the bomb had gone off. The houses looked quite a mess. Only doors and windows off, though, because there wasn't a house really near any of the three bombs. The nearest house to two of them would be at least a hundred yards away, and that was an isolated house down at the bottom end of Aberdeen Street, in between the first two bombs. We often wondered if there hadn't been a fourth bomb and it hadn't exploded, because the third bomb was so far away from the other two. But we never found out. They were quite big craters that they made.

We had seen the Zeppelins on previous nights caught in the searchlights, just like a big silver cigar. Seven or eight searchlights got them in the cone at the top and they were quite easy to follow really, nothing like the speed of today's aircraft.

One commodity we used to get as a supplement to sugar was called honey sugar. I presume it was so much of each. We used to have it on porridge oats and such like, or spread on bread. Butter and sugar were scarce. We never saw much meat. We used to grow so much of our own vegetables in the garden and we had our own poultry in the little bit of garden we had in the back yard.

One thing we used to eat — and it was surprising how nice they were — were boiled nettles. They were nice as a vegetable. Then we had dandelion instead of lettuce. That's eaten quite a lot today I think, especially in France. We used to grow a few potatoes. We had an allotment down at the bottom of Portobello Street so that helped a bit but it was two or three hundred yards to cart it home. We youngsters were better carters than my father so we had to do the carting. My father was a good foreman!

My mother was able to help a bit money-wise. She was a professional dressmaker and she used to make clothes for different people and through my father's firm, Maw, Till, Kirke's, she got a government contract for making poultices for the forces. That was a good job for us lads. There were three of us and we used to wind in turn till our arms ached. Mother had an old hand machine — she just used to feed the linen into the machine. It was probably in 25 or 30 yard lengths, and she would stitch it and then it went away and more would come for her to make up. It was all in best linen. With my father working at Maw, Till, Kirke's we were able to get clothes cheaper than other people. If we paid cash we got a discount and on top of that we got them at cost price. It made us really well dressed, what with that and the things that mother could make for us.

MRS LATHAM

I always remember going for green tea. I don't know why they called it green tea, but it was extra good tea. We used to have to go queueing before we went to school. Then if you were late for school, well that was just too bad. We didn't know what meat was. We used to have to have cod heads. A fellow used to come round and shouted, 'Fish all alive! Fish all alive!' You could get rabbit maybe if you queued. Of course, people were much poorer in the first war than the second. Money was very short. Poverty was a lot worse. Clothes were expensive so you used to make your own and make do. If there was a big family of you, clothes could be passed down. That's how you had to manage, or go without.

Zeppelins were just like a great long sausage and when they were in the searchlights you could see the men inside, because they got that low, just above the chimney stacks. And they sounded horrible — a real horrible noise as they were coming over. Still you could keep up with them because they didn't seem to move very quickly. They were very slow moving. If we saw one at the top of the street we could be at the other end of the street — running away from it. They were very big, an awful big size. They were sort of an egg shape, bigger at one end, not a lot but just slightly. But it was a lovely sight to see them trapped in the searchlights, and every time they moved the searchlights moved with them. Then you would hear bang, bang, bang — firing at them. If it hadn't been so dangerous you could have just stood and looked at them. Which I did, of course, because I didn't feel nervous of them. I didn't know what they were, or what would happen and I stood pointing up at them. My Dad and my Mam were shouting, 'Come on, come in.'

I often wished I'd kept things like the souvenirs when my brothers came home and those old cards they sent home.

When my four brothers came home on leave Mam said to me, 'You're not going to school. You're going out with the lads.' I said, 'Oh, I'll have to.' 'No, you're not.' So when my friend came to the door to see if I was ready, she said, 'She's not coming today. Tell the teacher all her brothers have come home on leave.' So I went out with my brothers.

The youngest one joined under age. When he went to the recruiting office they said to him, 'Walk to the pier and then come back and tell us your age again.' So he did and then they passed him. He went to France with the next oldest brother and they were in the firing line together. My youngest brother put his arms up and he was shouting for his Mam. My other brother wrote home and said, 'If you don't get our George out of the army, I will, because I'm not going to fight alongside of him.' So my Mam got him out, but he was only home a few months before he went back again. The brother who got him out was a soldier through and through, but the older one wouldn't have the army at all. He never got any further than Staffordshire — that was his billet, and he never got any further. I don't think in the whole time he did a full week's training because he was always at home. He was always having red caps after him, two at the top of the street, two at the back, waiting for him.

My brother-in-law never came back at all. He was in the Bantams. He went to France and never came home again, never saw his family. Their little boy was born after he'd been killed so he never saw him. They would just send a telegram to let you know they were missing. If your letters stopped you could write to the War Office and they would inform you if they were reported missing. We never got to know what really happened, not from the War Ministry. But a friend of his came home on leave and he said he saw them get blown up, blown to pieces. Whether that was true or not we don't know really. His wife got a war pension for him. He was such a jolly sort of chap as well. He could sing. We used to sit at the fireside when he came to see my Mam, and he would play the accordion and sing all the old fashioned songs. It was really nice.

After the war we had a great big party with tables all down the street and decorations. I used to have a photograph where I had one of my brother's uniforms on — all the young lasses got dressed up in uniform. We had all the windows and the doors decorated, and the particular terrace where I lived was nearly filled with relations and there was a great big blank wall. My eldest brother chalked and painted on it the King and the Queen and Union Jacks. It lasted ever such a long time.

MRS THELMA SYMMONS *[born in 1900 in Newland Avenue, Hull. Interviewed in 1982 in Beverley, where she still lives.]*

I was just 14 years old when the war started.

We lived on Newland Avenue in Hull. I remember very well that the bath was in the scullery — of course, bathing was a very cold business! A stone floor with linoleum in the kitchen, but the front room was carpeted and quite comfortable. Heating was coal fires, and I think we had a gas ring to boil the kettle on. The lavatory was just outside. The bath was covered over in the scullery and every Friday night it was opened up for us all to have a bath. During the week I think we kept all kinds of rubbish in there!

I went to Newland Avenue Girls School. When we lived in Beverley before this I went to Holland House School, which was right opposite where the post office is now. The Headmistress at Newland said it was a good thing I moved because she was appalled by my ignorance when I first went there. Of course, at the Holland House School we learnt just how to be little ladies and very little else. That was a private school — it was called Miss Stephenson's and was run by three very old ladies. They were always very fond of me because with my father going to sea he used to bring them all sorts of things back when he came home, such as scent *etc.* But everything I learnt I learned at Newland Avenue Girls Schools. We moved there about 1912, or 1911. When I first went, the Headmistress, Miss Wilkinson, gave me a paper of questions which I answered to the best of my ability, but, when I came to leave school, the Headmistress used to have the girls in to have a talk. She told me that, when she read the paper I gave in, she was 'appalled at my ignorance'. I never forgot that. That was a council school and I certainly had a better education there than at the private Holland House School as far as actual knowledge was concerned. Reading, writing and arithmetic were drilled into you at Newland. I don't remember ever being punished, but the Headmistress was a wonderful woman, very strict, but I don't think any of us would risk offending her! There was a boys' school there as well, but we were always kept apart, even at playtime.

Before my father was killed in 1916 he decided that I should go to Woods College, on Spring Bank. He paid for a year's education there, shorthand, typing and bookkeeping. I suppose he realised that, if something happened to him, I was the eldest and would have to do something about it! I remember he left the sea for a little while and went to Hornsea where he and some friends ran a rest home for soldiers. It was doing alright as well, but suddenly he got the fever to go back to sea and he couldn't do anything else — he just went! This was during the war — at the very beginning. He'd been going to sea ever since he was about 10 or 11 and he couldn't resist the call to go back. He was in the Merchant Navy and he was in a ship coaling the fleet of Scapa Flow. A telegram came one day to say that the ship had been blown up and nobody was saved.

This had an effect on our lives. The pension that my mother was given was a poor one and for my two sisters she was given just 10/- a week for each one. So it was a good thing I had learned shorthand and typing *etc.* and I started working at the Picture Playhouse in Beverley. Before my father went back to sea the last time he'd brought me over to Beverley from Hull and we went to see Ernest Symmons at the Picture Playhouse. I don't know how my father came to know him but he did, and I remember him saying to Ernest, 'Well, if anything should happen to me will you keep an eye on my family?'

When the telegram came that day to say my father had been killed, I later thought of going to see Mr. Symmons to see if he could get me a job. He said he thought it would be a good idea if I worked for him at the Picture Playhouse. He was only there every other night and his partner was there the other nights. It didn't take me very long to get into the business itself.

In fact, when I was about 18 I think I was running the place. I think I did everything but sign the cheques! We had an orchestra (a pianist, a cellist, a violinist and a drummer) and I remember the musicians were a bit crazy. If you paid them on a Friday night you weren't guaranteed to see them on a Saturday so we made Saturday payday.

The cinema was a family place. I think it was a place that everybody liked because it was a sort of 'speciality place'. The two men who ran it were so terrifically interested in that business and they were also cameramen. In fact, the raid on Scarborough was actually filmed by my husband, Ernest Symmons, and the BBC paid me for permission to show it. They have, in fact, paid me to show a few bits of film of ours. He lived in York and, as soon as it was known that Scarborough was being shelled, he went over to Scarborough and filmed all the damage and everything. I think he had a car then, because he owned a car almost before anyone else did. A Wolseley it was. Scarborough was shelled from the sea, a lot of damage was done, and the film he took was bought by one of the newsreels. When the BBC showed this film, I think Ernest still had the copyright — I know they paid me for showing it.

Yes, my mother used to get into a terrible state when the sirens went off. If we were in bed she'd get us up and take us out into the country. And I remember the night the Zeppelin came over and dropped a bomb on Edwin Davis's in Hull. My mother and I were asleep in bed and we heard the bombs going off and I think we immediately realised what it was and I remember distinctly going hot and cold. I'd heard of people going hot and cold but I definitely did so that night! I think they'd done an awful lot of damage in Hull, but after that my mother used to get us up and take us out into the country as soon as the sirens went. I don't remember them going very often, but I can definitely remember going into the country with my two sisters and my mother. My mother was really very afraid.

There were quite a few German shopkeepers at that time, pork butchers mostly, I think. I think they were rounded up very quickly. I mean, they weren't allowed to keep on running their businesses. There was a pork butcher on Newland Avenue but I don't recall having seen him, particularly after the Zeppelin raids — I think if people had seen him they would have murdered him.

I can remember the food getting poorer, we were very badly fed at that time. There was a shop in Beverley Road called Care's, and I remember being able to get a few scones there. All the bakeries had very poor stuff in.

After the war I can remember jobs being very scarce, there was a depression, everybody was hard up. During the war women were drivers and conductors on the buses.

I first went to work for my future husband when I was 16. He had an old Wolseley, and every now and again it used to go off with a terrific bang in the street and all the old ladies used to put their fingers in their ears and dogs used to fly! I used to catch the late train into Hull; then someone started a bus service towards the end of the war and I remember the return fare was 10d!

I can remember the hansom cab in Hull — I don't think there was one in Beverley. Of course, during the war we had an aerodrome here at the top of the Westwood and I got to know one of the officers who came from California. He'd gone up into Canada to join the Royal Flying Corps. It was the Royal Flying Corps in those days, not the Royal Air Force. The aerodrome was where the racecourse is. I'd never heard of Leconfield then, not till after the war. There were a lot of planes here in Beverley, though, for training as well as service. It was quite exciting having the aerodrome here because a lot of the personnel used to come down to the Picture Playhouse night after night — there was nothing much else to do, you know.

After my father was killed I went to work regularly at the Picture Playhouse, Beverley, and I soon got into the way of it, the booking of films and the running of the place generally. And if we were lacking in musicians I had to go into Hull to the musicians' union and engage people who were needed. The programme started off with a newsreel and then probably a short film — a comedy of some sort, and then the star film, which could be anything around an hour or an hour-fifteen minutes even. It was fitted with music — a musical score used to come with the film so the musicians had some idea of what to play, but when the talkies arrived life was very much easier because we could do without the musicians! There was another cinema in Beverley called the Marble Arch and my future husband came to an agreement with the Marble Arch that if they were going to put in talkie apparatus they would give him three months' notice. Well, he learned that the Western Electric apparatus was waiting at York station to come through to Beverley for them to install it. So, he said,, 'Well, I'll beat them to it.' And he'd been studying it for a long time and, before the Marble Arch opened with the Western Electric apparatus, he opened with his own apparatus which he had completely made and done himself! It was really wonderful, after quite a lot of experimenting and a lot of hard work put in by all the staff.

MR ALFRED AND MRS FLORENCE DEE *[Mr. Dee was born in Lincolnshire in 1903. Came to Hull in 1910 and lived in Mayfield Street. Mrs. Dee (née Mower) was born in 1906 in New George Street, Hull. Both interviewed in 1985 by Janet Harrison. Still live in Hull.]*

ALFRED: I was eleven years old when the First World War broke out. I was at Wawne Street School on Spring Bank. We had come to Hull from Lincolnshire in 1910 to a ten-roomed house at 68, Mayfield Street, off Spring Bank. We were a big family, eight brothers and sisters, and my father came to Hull to take a job as a commercial traveller for a biscuit firm in Glasgow. I had three brothers older than myself and they went in the Merchant Navy. They were only boys even then and, of course, I was not old enough for any kind of service.

When the buzzers first went it was very frightening. The buzzer was on Blundell's. Everybody had already been told to black all the windows out and we used to put out the gas lights in the street. I've done that myself: you just climbed up and pulled the arm down and it put the light out. People were so full of panic they urged you to turn the lights out in case the Zeppelins could see them. There was no bombing in the early part of the war. That didn't start until later. But there never had been any bombing at all before and people were very frightened.

FLORENCE: I don't know how we got to know, but people were told when the Zeppelins were still a long way off. They were so high in the sky that you could see them a long way off and, of course, they were too high to land the bombs where they wanted so they used to wait until dusk before coming in. When the warning came our mothers used to say, 'Take off your frock and your shoes and put them in a little parcel and get yourselves ready, so when they come we'll just go out in the fields.'

So you used to set off for the fields, where it was harmless. Mother had one child at one end of the pram and another at the other, a board across the pram and another one sat on there, and the others walking beside, because

Mrs. Dee, then Florence Mower, aged 12, is on the far right in the back row. There were two more children to come, making 13 in all!

there were six of us then. Mother had eleven altogether but there were only the six of us then.

I remember one night in particular. I had measles or some sort of infection. A Zeppelin came over and grandma and I, we all went out to the other side of the road, Lockwood Street, where there was Cannon Street Station, on the old Hull and Barnsley railway. There was a school yard there and we all tried to hide under the boards. People used to do that rather than stay in the houses because they were frightened of being buried in them if they were hit by a bomb. I was all wrapped up and Grandma carried me. We were standing there and we saw this silver shape and there must have been about a dozen searchlights on it. But it was too high up for our guns to reach it. In any case, the only gun we knew of was a wooden gun on the top of Blundell's.

When we got word that one had been sighted, mother used to get us all ready and we used to go to BOCM cake mills and down in their cellars. It was lovely and warm amongst the linseed bags and everything. I don't think I was ever frightened. Perhaps I was too young: I was only about eight years old. But you were certainly tired and didn't want to trail out yet again. When we didn't go to BOCM, we used to go down in King's old cellars. They were stone steps there so mother made us all take a cushion each to sit on, 'So you don't get king-cosh,' she used to say. There was quite a crowd of us, we six and mother and father and grandma. All the mothers and fathers would have a good chat and we got cups of tea brought round and so on. It really didn't seem frightening to me. Even in the last war I wasn't frightened. It seems a terrible thing to say, but I never even used to bother to go into a shelter. If the all-clear sounded before twelve o'clock, you went to school the next day. But if it was after twelve, you had a half day off. I used to hope it would be later because then we wouldn't have to get up in the morning.

ALFRED: The school authorities would know that you'd be tired out.

We had a great big gas cupboard at our home, about half the size of a normal room. My father used to bundle us all in there. One night there had been quite a lot of bombing and we had heard that a bomb had dropped in Hymers Avenue grounds. I went with two or three more lads and we saw this big hole. There was not much damage because this was right in the centre of Hymers College grounds. The crater was so big you could get a horse and cart in it. Bombing was still new and such a big hole seemed terrible to us, yet it would only be a fifty pound bomb.

FLORENCE: Against Holy Trinity Church, where the Labour Exchange is now, that used to be Edwin Davis's. It was a lovely shop, with a broad staircase to go up and floor-walkers brought you a chair as soon as ever you came in. It wasn't a case of picking and choosing for yourself. Everything was stored behind beautiful long counters and you didn't just pick what it was you wanted from the peg: you had clothes made. Even in what was Hammond's then, where they had ready-made clothes, they were stored in big wardrobes and they wouldn't let you go and see for yourself. They measured you and brought the garments to you. But I used to love going into Edwin Davis's with the floorwalkers coming up to meet you, 'Good morning, madam, which department did you want? Upstairs? Ah yes,' and he'd call one of the girls, 'See madam upstairs.'

But the shop was bombed and I remember going there with my sister and brother. There were rolls of cloth, all smoking, and rolls of ribbon. There was a policeman on duty and we asked if we could have some of the ribbon. He said yes and he'd reach it down for us. We got ever so much ribbon. It was all debris, really, and the policeman just let us take some.

ALFRED: The drivers and conductors on the buses were mainly young men. As the war went on more of them went into the forces and were replaced by women on the trams. In those days, if there was a young man in the street, the women would ask him why he wasn't in the army, when their sons had had to go.

FLORENCE: There were even young boys going. Once they were marching them down Spring Bank, with bands and everything. Some thought it was great but others didn't want to leave their mothers. Some, after all, were only about seventeen.

ALFRED: They used to march them from the barracks somewhere along Spring Bank down to the station and off for the Front. I played truant one day to watch.

By then the massacres had been so bad they were conscripting young men of seventeen. Now a boy of seventeen then was really only like a fourteen-year-old today, they had led such sheltered lives at home. They used to march them off with a band to put on a show and make them feel better. But this day, one of the young ones ran out of the ranks and tried to run away. It was terrible, really, taking young boys away from their mothers to be cannon fodder.

Food became short too, and my father was told to let his customers have only one tin of biscuits per month. Some of the salesmen would let anybody have them, just to get rid of the quota,

Mr. Alfred Dee, aged 23.

but my father stuck by the rule.

One of my brothers in the navy went on to minesweepers but another was on grain runs from America to England. By 1917 it was really serious and they were sinking one ship in three with the German U-boats. He was on a ship, I think from Baltimore in America, and they had got as far as the Irish Sea when they were torpedoed. Fortunately he survived right through the war. But a friend of my brother's, Len Bateman, who joined as a cabin boy at the same time, his ship was sunk on their first run to America and everybody was lost. They had started as cabin boys, quite confident that the war would be over in no time. That was the attitude of most people. There was widespread patriotism at the start — 'Oh, we'll kill the Germans.' Kids went in for that particularly. It was reinforced by fear of wondering what might happen to us if the Germans won the war.

FLORENCE: What frightened me was the German hats, those helmets with the spike at the top. That seemed more frightening than the soldier himself.

ALFRED: There was a pork butcher's shop on Spring Bank, Kress and Wagner's. They were from Germany. There were a lot of German pork butchers in England at the time, and quite a number in Hull. Rumours went round that Kress and Wagner were spies and, in fact, I was one of the lads that went and stoned the shop: a big gang of us under the trees that lined Spring Bank, chucking big stones through the windows. It happened all over Hull.

FLORENCE: There was a pork butcher's down Wincolmlee, Barmston Street, near where St. Silas' was. There was the shop downstairs and they had a piano upstairs. They broke all the windows and I can remember seeing the piano actually thrown through the upstairs window. Where the poor butcher and his wife and children were, I really don't know. They just raided them all. It was terrible.

ALFRED: There was one pork butcher in West Parade and I knew all the family. They were very nice people and on a Saturday night they used to fry sausages and other savouries, saveloys and so on, they were beautiful. You could get two or three for about threepence.

FLORENCE: Even if you saw somebody in the street that was a bit strange, somebody perhaps with a black beard, kids would run after them shouting,'You're a German spy.' Someone you hadn't seen near your terrace before, who just happened to be looking around, was automatically a German spy. Grown-ups as well as children were just the same with the Irish. Irish people were just spies for the Germans. We had some near us down St. Paul Street, Patsie Kelly and his housekeeper. Patsie used to wear one of these Catholic round hats, and they used to follow him and shout after him, 'Irish German spy.'

ALFRED: It had started up even before the war with people claiming that the German bands that used to go round giving concerts in the street were really going round spying. There were two light wooden planes that were often around in the sky. We never knew where they were stationed. One was flown by a German, his first name Herman, but I forget his second name. The other flier was an Englishman called Whitehouse. He came down nearby in 1912 and we went out to see what had happened and he said he had run out of petrol. But there were all sorts of rumours about Herman.

I myself left school in January, 1917, and I remember going down to the King George Dock to meet my brother. There was a coloured cook on the ship and I asked him if there was any chance of a job on the ship. He said they could do with a cabin boy. So I told my brother and he said, 'You're not coming on this ship. If she gets hit there'll be two gone from the family.'

My father saw an advert in the paper that Lady Middleton was at Beverley doing charity work, 'sewing socks for soldiers' was a phrase they used for it at the time. She lived in Birdsall House, near Malton. The advert was for a kennel boy and my father suggested I go and see her in Beverley. So I did and got the job and became a kennel boy among the fox hounds for Lady Middleton.

The job involved exercising the dogs with the whipper-in. He used to go in front with me behind them. He was on a horse but I was on foot and if one of the hounds strayed from the pack I had to chase after it and bring it back. Lord and Lady Middleton were quite old, approaching eighty, but both rode, he a small pony and she a mule. They were very pleasant and would come round and talk to you.

I was only there a few months before giving my notice in. She came to me and calling me by my Christian name asked why I was leaving. I explained that I didn't like the huntsman, who was rather a bully. She said they were going on holiday to stay with Lord Brownlow at Grantham. They had their train and took their own valet and other staff and she asked me to come as a butler's boy. So I went to Belton House with them. I only stayed there a few months because I didn't like the butler.

When I got back home I wished I'd stayed where I was, because out there in the country you hardly knew there was a war on. You never heard a word of bombs or anything like that. My father wasn't very pleased about it.

There used to be a big waggon works down here on Springhead Road. It was open country from Walton Street and the Hull and Barnsley Waggon Works. I met a lad who told me that they wanted some apprentice waggon builders at Springhead. So I went and got a job there. When I first started there it was a six o'clock start so you had to be up by five. If the buzzers had gone, and they went nearly every night, you were tired out, but you still went to work. And it was hard work. Looking back, you wonder how we managed it.

I hadn't been there long before they started women on painting the waggons. It was the first time women had been doing work like that. Some of them were even doing heavy work because this would be about 1918 and so many men had gone into the war and been killed that they had to take women. It had to be like that and we didn't think anything about it.

One of the men who did come back, and very few did, had been gassed. His neck was twisted permanently and I've often wondered how he managed such hard work, knocking the old waggons to bits and building a new one in its place.

FLORENCE: There was a lot of rejoicing on Armistice Day. We all got dressed up. I put mother's long dress on. We all went down into the town from Lockwood Street, into Victoria Square, and there was dancing and singing — *Keep the Home Fires Burning, It's a long way to Tipperary*, all those songs — we sang everything. I know we weren't very old, but everybody went swarming into the town. There were crowds of us. It was such a wonderful occasion that everybody was happy. There was dancing in the terraces. There were streamers put out and flags. There were parties, on long trestles, with the whole terrace contributing. Everybody brought their chairs out. It really was a joyous affair, lovely, with writing on the walls, 'Welcome home, Dad.'

ALFRED: There must have been about twenty terraces down Bean Street. Every one of them was decorated with bunting from window to window across the street. They were so happy, especially those whose sons or daughters were still alive. After all, millions had died and lots of people had lost their fathers, sons, husbands.

I spoke with some who did come back and from what they told me it must have been really terrible in those trenches, full of water, frozen to ice in winter. Some men were in those trenches not for days, but for weeks, until the frostbite was so bad they had to have their legs amputated. I knew one who had suffered with trench feet and his were completely covered in bandages for the rest of his life. In some cases their feet more or less fell off completely. Every day this man had to be bandaged before he could go out. He never got cured.

It was a terrible war; more terrible even than the second.

MRS CARRIE DAWSON [*née Johnson, born 1900 in Chapel Street, Scunthorpe. Interviewed by Maureen Fagan. Still lives in Scunthorpe.*]

I was sixteen or seventeen, and I worked at Hopper's in Barton on munitions, drilling holes in the noses of shells. We wore a cap to put your hair under. We had tunics with belts. It was the first time I'd ever worn trousers.

A girl picked up something from the road they'd just been tarring and threw it. A bit hit my eye and partly blinded me. I think that's why I'm having trouble now with my eyes. My father said I'd better go home and I had to because I was partly blind for six months.

My father worked in the pits and when there were air raid warnings we used to go to his cabin and sit there. It was nice and warm there. Of course, in the Second World War we had shelters but not in the First.

When the Zeppelin came over Barton we were out in the street. We had to get away from the factory. It came up the Humber. I was at home when the Zeppelin flew over Scunthorpe and killed five men. I don't think we looked up at it but bits of shell flew on to our window sills. We were frightened after that and we used to go out on to the moors where there were no buildings. They didn't come over a lot but they tried to find the works at Scunthorpe. We got a lot of sirens and warnings and what have you.

I had two sailor brothers. My eldest brother was lost off the coast of Ireland. Nothing was found of the ship, the H.M.S. *Begonia*. He was going to marry a nurse and his banns had been read out at Scunthorpe Church for the first time on Sunday. We got the news on the Monday and we never heard anything more. My mother couldn't rest, not hearing whether he'd gone or not, until one morning she said, 'Don't worry any more because he's come to me and he's been found.' Years after, we were holidaying in Ireland and we went to Poole Harbour. The courier said we were passing a cemetery where a sailor boy was found. An actress was walking on the beach and she found this sailor boy. She had him buried in the cemetery we were passing. Something stopped my heart and I went like stone. I knew that my brother was buried there. We went back again. We had miles to walk. It just said, 'Some mother's son'. I am convinced my brother is there. We took a snap of it. His banns were read out three times at Scunthorpe Church.

We never knew what meat was. We never knew what a boiled egg was. My father used to have two, and we would sit round him while he cut the top off and we had it in rotation because there were ten of us.

MRS. ANNIE RALPH *[born 1892 in Cleveland Street, Hull. Interviewed in 1985 at Marfleet House by Tim Nicholl. She died in 1986.]*

My grandmother took me when I was only a little baby and I was brought up by her. My mother had twelve children but I didn't think of them as brothers and sisters. I can remember the celebrations at the relief of Mafeking. I had an uncle there who died of enteric fever.

During the First World War, when the bombing started, people used to break into the German shops and smash them up.

The first bombing was in town at Edwin Davis's warehouse. Troops were stationed in Edwin Davis's, my husband amongst them. They went from there to Preston near Hedon and then on to the Dardanelles. It was the East

Yorks. A lot of them had joined up for the bounty money because there was no work. When my husband joined up I was very poor, with two children to keep, a boy and a girl. I got a job with BOCM in Wincolmlee. They used to give me half an hour to get the children up. I went to several different mills. There were some men working there, conscientious objectors. We gave them no peace. The foremen were still working. They were quite good though one man was hostile towards us women. But we were not taking men's work. We were doing men's work to help the war effort.

We used to work from six in the morning till five at night and we got good wages. I really furnished my home from what I earned. It was heavy work, barrowing and loading lorries, but the atmosphere was friendly. Then I went on a machine, cleaning and purifying linseed oil. We used to wear clogs and overalls. It was a bit noisy but I enjoyed working there.

My father was a docker. There was no work then just as it is now. He was a territorial and was one of the first to join up. He joined up under Colonel Shaw for the bounty money, thinking there would not be a war. He was just short of money. Five shillings when there was work but nothing if there was none. He had one leave out of the trenches and told my husband not to join up. He said it was hell.

But in 1916 my husband joined up with the East Yorks. That was after my father had been killed at Ypres. He was at the Dardanelles and then in France where he got wounded. He was a Catholic, though I was not, and he had a prayer book in his pocket. The bullet went right through the prayer book and into his arm. That was when he was recommended for a medal.

MRS. AUDREY WATERS [interviewed in 1985 in Kirkella by Janet Harrison, and has since died.]

I was fifteen in the June and the war started in August.

We admired the boys who joined up, little realising how horrible it was going to be. My brother joined up in September, 1914, on his seventeenth birthday. He was five feet eleven and a half and they accepted him in the Commercial Battalion. My mother expostulated with him because she wanted him to join the Fourth East Yorks, who were the territorials. He said he would go and join the Guards. So they left him alone. Perhaps it was as well, because he did come through the war. Whereas, if he had joined the Fourth East Yorks, he would probably have been killed like hundreds of other Hull boys.

It was amazing to see any hall that was of any size — there was a big one on Beverley Road that had been a skating rink — filled with soldiers. Every available space that could be taken up by troops was. Newland High School on Cottingham Road had been newly completed and was about to open but it was taken over and used as a hospital. As a young girl, I used to be taken there to sing to the troops, poor beggars. A captive audience if ever there was. My mother was very good hearted and she used to say that they did not want pretty girls in the kitchen; they wanted them where they could see them.

She herself was a voluntary helper in the kitchen and she kept a bag of white flour and she used to bake batches of teacakes and send me down to the hospital with them to give them to old soldiers who had nobody to visit them. I used to take these along on Sunday afternoons so they would have a bit of something extra for tea. There were wards of beds, one after the other, but I don't remember seeing any very drastic cases. They were all able to sit up in or beside the bed. There were a lot of V.A.D.s and some professional nurses. The V.A.D.s had a grey uniform and starched white apron down to their ankles and black stockings. Absolutely no glamour at all, not like we think of nurses today, in short frocks and little caps.

In those days you didn't go into a shop unless you were going to buy something. I remember Hammond's putting a notice in the newspaper and hanging it up in their new shop, 'Walk round and you will not be pressed to buy.' That was the beginning of this open shop system. Traditionally you only went into a shop to buy something and you were very embarrassed if you walked out without having done so. You were met at the door by a floorwalker who very often wore a frock coat. They would say, 'Yes, madam?' and take you to a shop counter, pull out a chair for you to sit down (I've done this with my mother many times), call a girl and say, 'Madam wants so and so,' and you were attended to and shown out of the shop afterwards. There was none of this hectic scrambling for goods as there is today. Some foods were in short supply during the war. White flour became scarce and I can remember my father coming in and telling us there was a queue outside Maypole on Princes Avenue because they had some margarine. Mother put on her hat and hurried down to join the queue.

I can remember the first air raid. They dropped a bomb on Edwin Davis's which was where the Labour Exchange is now, opposite Holy Trinity Church. My brother was home on leave at the time and in uniform so he said they would let him through. He rushed down and helped the firemen. For two or three days afterwards he couldn't speak because he was so hoarse from the smoke. I think also there was a bomb that killed some people in a street called Campbell Street.

MRS EVA RIGGS *[born 1900 in Hunslet. Interviewed in Scunthorpe in 1985 by Maureen Fagan. Now lives in Appleby.]*
I was just 14 to 18 in the first war, and I had five brothers. Three went and one was killed and two came back. One was a sailor, the younger one, and

the other one was a soldier. Them two came back. The one that was killed was a twin. He was killed in the Dardanelles. My mother had twins and the other one died at three days old.

I lived in Hunslet. I was an orphan at ten. My mother and father died with ten months between each other. My mother had had a fall they told me afterwards and it paralysed her. I can never remember my mother taking me out. She was always in bed.

When I got to be sixteen, I begged my eldest brother who was married, and they brought their home to ours and we all lived together. I was brought up to go to Sunday School and all that rigmarole. They were a bit on the strict side with me. I hadn't to swear or knit on a Sunday. However, they weren't cruel to me. I had good meals. My sister-in-law was a good cook. Happen that's why I'm as well today — because I had good meals.

I watched the conductresses on the trams and kept thinking I would love to be a conductress. My brother said, 'No, you're not going — with late nights and coming home late, and besides they won't have you at sixteen!' You were supposed to be twenty one. When I was seventeen I was working in a jam factory and every day I said to my brother, 'Let me go! I'm seventeen now!' I went and had an interview. I filled a form in and I put that my age was seventeen. However, when the chap came to look at my form he said, 'You have to be twenty one!' 'Oh,' I said, 'I did want to try. It would be helping the war.' I went on and on. In the end he agreed to make a false entry and put twenty one. So I was on the trams till the war was over. They didn't turn us off straight away because the boys had to come home and take their jobs.

I loved it. We used to get up at four early turn and I've taken a load of miners on my tram — as many as I could get to the pit for the five o'clock shift. It used to be packed. The fare was three ha'pence — a penny and a ha'penny. Not one miner wanted change. They all had their three ha'pence ready. Their wives used to pack them up and put their three ha'pence at the side of their lunch.

We had a day off each week. We worked Saturday and Sunday so that was six days, but if somebody didn't turn up for an afternoon shift and you'd just gone into the depot to take your tickets in, they'd say, 'We want you to do this afternoon's shift. So and so hasn't turned up.' If you did a double shift that earned you a lot of money. I worked from five o'clock till eleven at night many a time during the war. As soon as I got in I used to fall asleep.

Food was scarce but those that were in uniform who were doing their bit were allowed to go in first if there was a queue. There used to be queues just for two ounces of butter, one egg, a bit of cheese or two ounces of bacon.

Once when I was on the trams we were in town and the sirens went. When they went everything stopped, no matter what. Even the travellers couldn't get off. They had to wait until that siren went again for all clear. But there was no bombing.

MR. JOE HUNTER *[born 1907; interviewed in 1985 by Tim Nicholl at Wold Haven Home, Pocklington, where he still lives.]*

I was still at school in Pocklington when the war started. I had five brothers and three sisters. There are only two of us left now, myself and an older sister. Three of my brothers were in the war. Two of them were in the East Yorks and the oldest was in the Royal Engineers. The middle one was invalided out of the army in 1917 because of trench feet. He lost all his toes through frostbite but he still managed to play football when he came out.

The youngest went out to India and, of course, he didn't get any home leave. But at the end of the war a lad called George Smith came and told my mother that he was back and had arrived at Pocklington station. My brother wasn't too pleased because he had meant to just walk in and take my mother by surprise. He had caught malaria in India and still used to have bouts of it from time to time. All three of them worked on the railway, following after my father.

We didn't have an air-raid siren here in Pocklington. Instead, the police used to go around with a first warning. A second warning meant that Zeppelins were approaching. We lived just outside Pocklington, at Burnby, and on the second warning people used to leave and come out to Burnby and our house used to be full of them. There was an old man called Billy Birkett who had an old Ford Lizzie motor car. He owned the field opposite our house. One morning after one of these warnings, I was off on my way to school and there he was with his car at the field. He was just getting in the car as I came by and he said, 'Now, young man, d'you want a ride?' I was quite surprised because he wouldn't speak as a rule. A miserable old devil he was. I wondered what on earth had come over him this morning but I accepted and got in the car. There was a cash box on the seat and he said he had just come back for it. 'We was down here last night, me and the wife, in them there sheds and I went and forgot the cash box when we went home.' One night we were out there and could see flames in the sky to the north. People were jumping up and down shouting that they'd hit a Zeppelin. Next morning we found it had been one of our own planes that had been shot down.

MRS GLADYS ALLEN *[née Johnson; born 1902, in Beaufort Street, Grimsby. Interviewed in 1985 by Maureen Fagan. Now living in Scunthorpe.]*

I was twelve years old when the First World War broke out. My father died in 1918, the day after Armistice. We lived in Gainsborough. My father was a boilersmith at Marshall's.

He was a Newcastle man in the regular army and my mother met him at the Tower of London. They were courting for eight years because he had a seven-year tour of duty in India. He came from a big family, because there were twenty-three of them and twenty-two of them grew up to be men and women.

The day they declared war, my father went to Grimsby to enlist. He was on the regular reserve so he went straight in and that was the last we saw of him for over a year. We didn't even know where he was.

His first action was in the retreat from Mons, and during it somehow he got caught up in the barbed wire, and when he eventually did get home I remember he showed me his back with the scars on it where the wire had torn him. He said there were good and bad amongst the Germans but he said he once saw a German officer chop the arms off a Belgian child. Further on the road there were a lot of German prisoners and the War Office Gazette printed a picture of a kind English soldier giving a German prisoner his last pipe of tobacco. That was my father. My mother used to send him out six clay pipes at a time. He used to chop the stems off short because that was how he liked them. He gave this German his pipe of tobacco and sent him on his way. The German gave my father a watch as a souvenir and my mother kept that for years.

Later he told me of the days without sleep in heaps of sludge they called trenches. They filled completely with water when it rained and with full

St. Thomas's Terrace, Campbell Street. The centre gap was No. 2 where three members of the Walker family were killed and one seriously injured, 6 June, 1915.

[Hull City Museums and Art Galleries]

packs on you could just slip back and fall in and just lie there till you died. They wanted to promote him but he wouldn't take any stripes because he said you lost all your friends.

Once, on leave in 1916, he met my mother's second brother. A complete stranger came up in Gainsborough market and said, 'I know you.' It was the only time I saw my father drunk. They went and got drunk and struggled home. We were out at the back in the ten-foot and we saw these two soldiers rolling from side to side. They were brought in as drunk as lords.

We managed reasonably while he was away, thanks to my mother who could make a meal out of anything. Ours was a two-bedroomed house with a front room downstairs and a kitchen, and a wash-house down in the garden. Some soldiers from Sheffield were billeted with us and we had to take them in whether we wanted to or not. My mother objected because there were only two bedrooms but they said the front room was big enough for four men. So they just put mattresses on the floor and we had four men with us.

The Ropery Road School was taken over by these soldiers and we were lucky in a way because these soldiers were good to us. I can remember going over to the cookhouse for some meat for my mother to cook. It was really stolen from the cookhouse but that didn't bother us — we were getting a good meal. I remember one whose people were butchers in Sheffield and they used to send great big parcels of food every week. Well, he didn't want it and he used to give it to my mother for us.

The soldiers used to say they were only here for a while because it would all be over in a week or two. My father spoke to some, once when he was home on leave, and told them it wouldn't be over for a long while. But they flatly denied it and said they were only out for a bit of fun. They hadn't had a pennorth of it by then.

We used to have to keep the lights out at night for air-raids and I can remember the Zeppelins. My mother had a big pram and she used to pack it up with things and always took her insurance policy with her. She'd also bring a loaf of bread and other food and a set of clean clothes. If the bombing got too bad in Gainsborough, we had to walk to Nottingham. So every night this pram was filled and put against the front door, so, if anything happened, all we had to do was open the door, out with the pram and off.

The Zeppelins used to follow up the Trent and were probably after the armaments at Marshall's or Rose's. There was also the T.N.T. factory. I remember the girls who worked there because of their yellow skins, almost tangerine. But we didn't have much trouble. I can remember one airship, because it was a wooden one. One big bomb landed at Morton and on the Sunday afternoon we all tramped over to have a look at the big hole it had made. It had blown half a house down and some apple trees were scattered on the ruin. We wanted to eat them but my mother told us not to touch them because they had been poisoned.

In 1915 a hospital for the war wounded was opened on the road to Morton. The soldiers who could manage were allowed out and I remember them coming down on their crutches and leaning against the wall on our ten-foot to light their pipes in the shelter from the wind. They were decent men and because they were locked in at certain times we used to go and pass them a bottle of beer through the railings. They would bring the bottles back the next day and we'd get a penny or ha'penny on the empty. My mother told them she wouldn't get them any more if they didn't bring the bottles back.

Later, when I was fifteen, I went to work at that hospital. I worked in the laundry, but I was very fond of children. I had helped bring all ours up. I used to sneak off the laundry and go and look after children in the wards. The sister asked me if I wanted to be a nurse, which I did. But I couldn't afford it because you had to pay to be trained and my mother needed my wages. So the sister asked if I wanted to try cooking instead of the laundry. So for six months I did all the cooking for the hospital with only a kitchen maid to help. At the end she said I should apply for the post as the hospital cook, so I did. They said I didn't have enough experience so I left.

Then, in 1916 when the first mustard gas was dropped, my father got gassed. He also got wounded in the hand. But he still went back after he got better though he got so bad that he was discharged. The gas really affected him badly. The only masks they had had were like those surgical masks, a piece of cloth with a pair of hooks on to go over the ears and hold it in place. That was no use in a full gas attack and he got so much it affected not only his lungs, but his stomach as well. When he was discharged he was very short of wind, his stomach was swollen and he was yellow. It was the gas that really killed him.

He went back to Marshall's but he could only do a brush job because of his crippled hand. There were six of us children then and we saw some of the terrible effects beside his physical wound. He used to have dreadful nightmares. He would wake up screaming even before he was taken ill. He was always fighting. Anything that moved, curtains, anything, he'd be getting up to fight. Yet, when he wasn't having nightmares, there couldn't be a nicer man.

He would go absolutely mad. I can remember it so well towards the end. He was in bed for a fortnight and he went raving mad. It was in my mother's bedroom and I can remember it so well. All she had in there was a full size bed and a gramophone with a big green horn at the window. We never knew why we took it upstairs. But if we had not, my father would have jumped through the window that night. He got out of bed and tried to strangle my mother and me. It ended with the horn going through the window. My neck went black with the marks where he had tried to choke me. He died the next day. The day after Armistice Day. We had no Armistice celebrations inside or outside the house.

After that my mother had the hardest life a woman could have had. My father had been in bed for the fortnight but we only had our own doctor for the first week. During the second week it was a relief man and he put on my father's death certificate, 'Not aggravated by war service.' Yet our own doctor was treating him for poison gas. So my mother got no war pension.

Soon after, I was thirteen and was allowed to leave school, when I got a job at 2/6 a week for working from eight in the morning till five at night. I was helping with the housework before I went out in the morning to look after an old lady in a wheel-chair all day. Seven days a week for two and sixpence!

My father actually should have had the V.C. He was in the First Lincolnshire. In France he had gone out of his trench, over the top to rescue a young officer. The Germans didn't fire at him because, my father said, the Lincs were good to the Germans and they knew it. So they didn't fire their guns but they pelted him with stones. He carried that officer back in full view yet no-one fired and a single shot would have been enough. He got him safe and he was recommended for the V.C. But he never got it. All my mother got was a letter and a little bronze box from the Queen.

She had to work hard. She took in washing and a bit of sewing. I used to bring it in and take it away in the dark at night, because she was on parish relief. That was ten shillings for my mother, five shillings for me, but only a shilling for the others. Thirty shillings a week my mother had to bring us all up. So she had to keep it quiet, because if she earned a shilling they took it off her money when she went next week. That went on until we were fully grown up. Until I got married I was having to help to keep the younger ones.

You got no help in those days.

MR. JACK ELLIS *[interviewed in 1985 in Scunthorpe. He died in 1987.]*

I joined up when I was seventeen, but I was in the army only for the one day, because my firm got me out and brought me back home. There was a committee that decided that the work I had been doing was more important than what I might be doing in the army. Actually I wanted to go in the navy. But I didn't do any service at all. My work involved diesel engines for submarines. The firm was based in Gainsborough. There were Marshall's and Rose Brothers. There were some special small submarines that were built locally.

I remember seeing Zeppelins. When they went over at night you could see a dark black shape in the sky. They did drop some bombs, but they missed the gasworks. People used to collect bits of shrapnel from the bombs dropped. We had a specimen on our mantelpiece for about a year.

Some people went into the fields for safety but we just got under our big oak dining table. One bomb was close. In fact we thought it had dropped in our garden, because we could hear debris from the crater falling on our roof. But in fact it had dropped about two hundred yards away. It was frightening.

People used to grumble about various things like the restrictions on licensing hours and rationing. You might be allowed four ounces of beef or whatever and not a fraction more. I remember my mother having to make do with tinned milk that you had to dilute with hot water. We didn't starve, but the German submarines meant there were all sorts of shortages: a lot of the ships carrying food from Canada were sunk. There were shortages in business as well. I was a draughtsman but I used to order timber and other materials for models. But they would just allow you the bare minimum of wood, not a bit more. Whatever it was, you had to order it absolutely nett.

My father was a fitter with Marshall's and my mother looked after the house but a lot of women started to go out to work. It was the first time that women had worked in engineering. They worked on turning and drilling. The shop was full of women. Most of them left after the end of the war, but some stayed on and had a good job. One even became a forewoman. It was the first time ladies had been in engineering and she was one of the top ones and was very clever at it.

I had friends in the army and navy but there were also conscientious objectors. They got black looks and were sent to Coventry, shouldered off. Some of them were sent to prison, mainly with short sentences of perhaps six months. There were quite a number against the government. It was a rough time to live through.

I remember Armistice Day. There was a hell of a show all over the country. People went mad. All night street parties, with beer and drinks and singing.

EMMA KEEITCH *[née Shepherdson; interviewed in 1985 by Janet Harrison. She still lives in Hull.]*

I was born on 30 November, 1894, in a small terraced house in Waterloo Street. My dad was Edward Shepherdson and my mother Christina, née Kitson. They had three children in three years and eight months, myself, Joseph and Edward. (More children followed later.)

I think the first thing I remember (we were then living in Park Road, near Pearson Park) was my mother rushing upstairs as some clothes were on fire in the living room. She put Joe and Ted under each arm and I had to put my arms around her neck and hold fast. I remember my mother rushing to a house at the other side of the terrace and sitting us all on a couch and warning us not to move. I think we were too frightened to move — after all, we were only babies.

I think the next thing was going to Park Road School, sitting on forms and writing with pencils and slates. And woe betide you if you made a mistake. You got a sharp rap on the back of your hand with a ruler. My two brothers also went to the school with me. I would be about four, Joe three and Ted just turned two, but we all had to learn: no playing with toys then. My brothers had frocks and pinafores on as the boys were not put into trousers until they were four or five years of age, and then it was a big occasion.

Soon after, we moved into Clyde Street. A thing I remember so well was someone shouting, 'Mafeking has been relieved!' I was six or seven but I can still recall the street was in an uproar.

The following year a cousin of my mother's came to our house dressed in a red coat and black trousers with white stripes up the sides. He brought me a little black doll, Joe a small violin, and Ted a tin whistle. I remember later being out with my mother and seeing him in the street selling matches — matches or shoe laces and boot blacking. Many old soldiers did that kind of thing or formed tin whistle bands and sang in the street. There were also what we called German bands, about six or seven of them playing in the street, collecting money. He ended up in the workhouse where, I'm afraid, many soldiers from the Boer War ended their lives.

When we lived in Clyde Street, we used to come up Hessle Road in a waggonette, a horse-drawn vehicle with seats on either side facing each other with a single step up into the body of it. It used to cost twopence for

Victory Parade passing City Hall, Hull.   *[Christopher Ketchell Collection]*

adults and a ha'penny for us. When we got out at Victoria Square, as it is now, we had to walk on to my grandmother's because we couldn't afford a further ride.

After that there were the horse buses. I don't remember a lot of them but then came the electric buses with open tops. You got wet sitting up there if it rained. Then trolley buses. We never thought they would work because they had to have wires. All that was much later, of course.

At that time there were green fields beyond the Avenues in the north of Hull and Spring Bank finished at the railway at Walton Street. Beyond that, where Willerby Road is, was all country.

The house I was brought up in had a front room, living room, a very small scullery, two bedrooms and an attic. There was a back yard and in it we had a copper with a fire under to heat the water for washing. There was also a petty and the dustmen used to shovel the muck into tins to empty it. Later they put a tin underneath so they could just lift the tin out. We were there a long time before they put water lavatories in. There was the petty at one side, the coal house at the other and the back door and they all met together — it was only a small yard. In the scullery was a small brown clay sink and we were lucky because we had a tap inside as well as outside. When we went into the house in 1910 there was still no gas there so my parents had it put in in the living room, the front room and the bedroom. For anything else we used candles and, as the stairs went up between the room and the passage, they were pitch black. When my father was ill in bed we had candles on the landing to light us up and down.

The front was furnished with a couch, four chairs, two large easy chairs in each corner and a polished table in the middle. There were pictures on the walls, oil paintings, photos and things and underneath long frames which held six photos. There wasn't a spare inch. There was a large window with four panes with lovely lace curtains and venetian blinds. I used to bless those when I had to wash them every week. The fire place had wooden carved uprights at the side with a mantel-piece on top, covered with ornaments. The grate was rather low and under it was an ashpan. There was a big brass kerb raised up at each end; at one end there was a poker and shovel and at the other some tongs. They were supposed to be for picking up fallen ashes, but, of course, they were never used for that. They were all solid brass and took some cleaning. A fire was lit every Sunday, so Monday was quite a job. When we spring cleaned it took well over a week to take all the pictures and ornaments down to wash, and the venetian blind all taken to pieces, all the laths and tapes washed and put together again. Now, you wonder how we did it all.

The other fire, in the living room, had a range at the side. There were bars across the fire itself and the top three of them were hinged, so you could drop them to form a tray for the kettle and pans to stand on — there were no gas or electric ovens then. At one side of the fire was a lid which must have covered a container for hot water. But it was cracked and we only used it for firewood, ready chopped, to keep it dry for lighting the fire in the morning. On the other side was the oven. The fire and oven were raised so there was space for ashes underneath to be raked out and at the top was a flue out of which you could scrape the soot. There was a similar opening on the other side of the oven to brush out soot from there as well. You cleaned these out and collected any re-usable cinders every day, and black leaded the grate itself every week.

We bought litle blocks of black lead made by Reckitt's. You mixed this with water on a spare tin lid or whatever was handy, spread it all over the grate, bars and so on and then worked on it with another brush until you could see your face in it. If you could spare a soft duster to finish it all off, so much the better. The hearth was then washed over with a cloth dipped in whitening. Then the fender had to be black leaded. The poker, shovel and tongs all had to be polished with emery paper — they were steel. There was also a brass stand with a full-size copper kettle which had to be cleaned with Brasso. A good three hours' job, but it looked lovely when finished.

The weekly wash was another big job. We used to dolly the tablecloths and pillow cases — they were all cotton then. They were brushed inside and outside. I used to wet and dolly them and give them to my mother to brush on the table. By the time she had done that I'd done the towels and teacloths with a second dollying and put them in the boiler. Then I'd dolly the shirts and collars ready for brushing. Then it was getting the other things out of the boiler and into cold water and into the bath tub for rinsing. So it took four waters to get through the different batches. After they were rinsed, we put them in water again with some blue in it and then we put them through the wringer. Then we made up the starch rather as you make custard now and we would starch pretty nearly everything — pillow cases, sheets, tablecloths, pinafores, blouses, shirts, collars. We had about six lines right across the living room and we hung the sheets up at night. We took those down in the morning and hung the rest of the washing in their place. There was also a brass rod across the mantelpiece and that was always full with drying things. There was a clothes horse as well, because it was a very big wash with so many in the family and four beds going.

My mother used to make brimstone and treacle. You used a pound of black treacle and mixed brimstone, it would be sulphur then, in it and stirred it well up. We were all lined up for a spoonful of it every night, before we went to bed. It was supposed to clean the blood, but, believe me, when we went to the lavatory you could smell it a mile away.

As time went on, we grew up and started work. Ted was apprenticed to a bricklayer. Joe went out to work, as we thought, and we never saw him again for years. My mother's hair turned white overnight. If you wanted to work in the big shops like Maw, Till, and Kirke's or Marris, Willows and Smith's that was in Carr Lane, you had to pay to be apprenticed as a milliner or counterhand. You got no money for five years while you learnt all about it.

But I started work in a brewery. Every dinner time my mother left out a stone of flour in a bowl and I kneaded it up for bread for mother to bake at tea-time. The brewery was Moore and Robson's in Raywell Street. They'd had boys there but they had been getting drunk, so they had started setting girls on. They had to be eighteen. We used to sit four round a machine. One would put the bottles on as it turned; another would take them off; a third would put them under a screw to screw the top on and the fourth would put them into a box and take them away. We couldn't leave that machine, because everybody would be stopped unless we could get somebody who was walking through to take our place while we went to the lavatory. And you worked four or five hours non-stop at that.

Before we did that, we used to push great big barrels of beer up onto the gantries and the man then flooded them all into a pipe. And there was bottle washing. The water for that was bitterly cold. One would put the bottles onto the conveyor so they were filled with water. Another would take them off and a third would put them into crates. That was another job on which nobody could leave the machine unless someone would take their place.

We got eight shillings a week, seven in the morning till half past five at night, five days a week and seven to twelve on a Saturday. We wore overalls and clogs because the place was always soaking wet from bottling machines. Eventually I got upstairs, delivering to the lorries. We used to load it on to a conveyor belt that took it downstairs. I had the orders to fill up and send down to the lorries.

The younger drivers had joined up at the start of the war, so there were only the older men left as drivers. By about 1915 beer itself was in short supply, so the brewery only delivered to their own houses. Any private pub or club had to come to the brewery to collect their orders. I've seen them come with handcarts, cars, all sorts lined up down Raywell Street waiting to be served. But they could only have four boxes at a time, each one holding two dozen bottles, and I've had many a sovereign offered me if only I would let them have another box. But I wouldn't have taken their money and I couldn't possibly have done it anyway. I'd have been rich if I'd been able to.

I was eighteen then and had started courting a boy called Frank but we had to be in by ten, though he was allowed into my home. This was still early in the war. My mother and father and Frank and I had gone to some friends in Cleveland Street when the air raid siren sounded. It was one continuous sound and it got on our nerves so we decided to come home. The blackout was in force but the search lights were sweeping the sky as we came down Cannon Street. We could see the guns and soldiers on the roof of Rose, Downs and Thompson's. They were certainly there, as Frank worked at Cannon Street station and saw it put up. We got home but the siren was still going when we decided to go to bed.

No-one was worried when we heard a bang. We all rushed upstairs and had our heads out of the attic window, when we saw Edwin Davis's (a big shop in town) go up in flames. Two or three other fires flared up. When we got to know the next day that it had been bombs we never went into the attic again. But the greatest shock of all was that the guns on top of Rose, Downs were wooden guns. What a commotion that caused even to this day. Only last year there was an argument in the *Hull Daily Mail* about it. A lot of people said it was on Blundell's corner at the end of Spring Bank. But I am absolutely sure it was Rose, Downs because of Frank working opposite it. It had soldiers in uniform and there were searchlights going round it.

Ted joined up at sixteen. Father could have reported him because he was too young. But he would have found some other way as everyone wanted to have a good time while it lasted because nobody believed it would last until Christmas. We had other raids, including one at Scarborough, when a German ship bombarded the town one morning, causing a lot of damage and quite a few deaths.

Whenever the soldiers or their friends came home on leave, mother generally managed to bake and make sandwiches so we had many a lovely time singing round the piano or playing games, postman's knock, winking, fruit games. No drink, in fact, you could hardly buy it — it was so scarce. We had some lovely nights. I had three brothers by then and when they or their friends came home we always had a party. Among the songs we sang were *When the Boys Come Marching Home; Home, Sweet Home; When We Come Back to Blighty*. There were hundreds of songs we sang at those parties and we would just go through them, moving from one to another, one to another. And the games! Postman's knock — we just loved to go to the door, or just outside, just for a kiss. We used to long for somebody, just for a kiss. And we'd think of that for ages. In the winking game, if the boy happened to pick you, then he kissed you and it was then your turn to pick the man. It was a smashing game.

In the fruit game, you all had a fruit, any fruit, and the one in the middle used to shout, 'Apple, apple, apple!', as quickly as you could. If you had an apple, you had to shout, 'Apple!' before whoever it was had finished. Anyone who knew the game used to pick blackcurrant because you would always get that word in before they finished the three.

One day in 1916 a soldier went to my grandma's shop (my dad's mother) and said he had been talking to Joe, the brother who had simply disappeared three years previously. A group of them had been coming home on leave and this man had asked his name, and he had said it was Joe Shepherdson and he had then got out at a country station. The young man had asked the others if they knew what regiment this Joe Shepherdson belonged to and where it was stationed. When father got to know, he wrote to the officer explaining things and asking if it would be possible for Joe to have extra leave to come home. Joe did come home next day, but my father had warned us all not to say a word about the missing three years, so we never did find out where he'd been. He was in the war to the end and won a Military Medal and bar, and after that first return he always came back to us for leaves and shared the good times.

Strangely enough, another brother, Charles, was in a house in Market Weighton when he saw Joe's photo, in uniform, on the sideboard. When he asked who it was he was told that it was a boy who had gone to work on the farm until he had joined up and they thought he must have been killed in the war. Charles didn't say anything but was disappointed that Joe had not let them know, but there may have been a reason. Ted, who joined at sixteen, did go to France, but they found he was too young so they returned him to England, but still in the army. When it first started, there weren't enough uniforms and a lot of them had to train in their own clothes. It was a long time, nearly till Christmas, before they got any kind of uniform at all — long, short, anything. Frank and my brother were in the East Yorkshires.

There was a small picture place near us. It cost us fourpence, which was a lot of money then. We used to go mainly for the Pathé News, that was the real show, the war and people going away or coming back.

More and more men were lost in the war. Family after family were wiped out, because if one man — boys as they were then — joined up, the whole family joined up, until in 1917 and the beginning of 1918, every man, young or old, was called up. Frank, the boy I had got engaged to, had been let off because he was the only one left at home to look after his mother and he also worked on the railway. But he was among the last to be called up. He had only three months' training and then was sent out to the Front. Six months later he was dead, with thousands of others who were sent into the Big Push, as they called it, utterly unprepared. He, like a lot more, was only reported missing, and like them was never heard of again to this day. I didn't get to know about Frank until some time later, because his mother and sisters thought I had no business enjoying myself at home at the parties for my brothers when he was missing. I was there, happily waiting news of him, never dreaming he was lost.

So, quite unaware, we joined the Armistice festivities. My mother collected for it — she was a runner and joiner, you know — and we borrowed forms from the school and had them all down the middle of the road (there wasn't much traffic then) and hundreds of kiddies were seated there, all dressed up. The committee had got a nine-gallon barrel of beer in our room for the men. I remember a gentleman at the end, a business man, who came into our house — it was open door for us — and they found him lying under the tap drinking from it. They had to carry him home. We had decorated the doorway with electric lights from the Christmas tree and we took the piano into the street and we kept the party going all night and all next morning. It was smashing, and smaller parties continued for a while as different ones got home.

Mind you, they talked about coming back to a country fit for heroes and there was no work and there was no money and there was no help. Things were very, very bad.

MR. STAN HALL *[interviewed in Hull and is very well known as a sports commentator on local radio.]*

I was born in Fleetwood in 1908 and I didn't come to Hull until I was older. My father was a Jersey man and somebody had the idea that if they repaired the Jersey potato barrels in Fleetwood and sent them back to Jersey it would save time. So he came to Fleetwood, met my mother and settled down there. Then he went to Salford where I spent my early school life. Later I married a Hull girl and came over here.

My early life was a very happy one, my dad being a cooper in the Manchester market. He was a pretty enterprising bloke and watched how the salesmen sold their fruit. When the time came that he thought he could better himself, he applied for a job in the Manchester fruit market and spent the rest of his working life there with the exception of World War One, when like millions of other Englishmen he went to serve his King and Country. He did that in the 10th Battalion of the Lincolnshire regiment, known as the Grimsby Chums or the Grimsby Pals.

The school in Salford was All Saints Roman Catholic School. During the war half the schools were turned into military hospitals and the other half had to accommodate them. We shared with another school, and when we changed over with them, unless the teachers were on the job immediately, we used to call them 'Prody dogs' and they called us 'Cat Lickers' and some of the finest fights you ever saw in your life took place.

The school was interrupted by the war. Everybody wanted to get into it because it was going to be over by Christmas. Anybody who wasn't in khaki was a coward and the girls used to go round giving out white feathers. So schoolteachers and specialists, who today would be exempt because their work was of national importance, went into the army, so we lost all our teachers. Most of our education was given by student teachers, girls about 18 years of age and boys up to the time they went into the army. As far as possible they did try to give us a normal education.

Men who had won medals used to come round and tell us how much we could help them by doing odd jobs. We bought lavendar and the girls sewed it in small bags. Then the boys sold it for a penny and, once we'd got the money, we would buy a box of Woodbines. In those days they were sold in packets of five for tuppence in old money and then we took these round to the military hospital and asked Matron if we could serve them to the lads, and very often the Matron would say, 'Yes, would you like to take them to them', which was a wonderful experience. We dashed off to hand them to the lads. We were never allowed to go on a bad ward, of course, a bad ward I mean where men were gravely injured. These were all what I would term walking wounded, so we handed in these cigarettes and very often the lads would sit us on their knees and talk to us. We used to come out walking on air because all this was very romantic. But what I always used to feel sorry for was that those lads that were wounded had to wear a ridiculous heavy light blue uniform with white turn ups to their trousers, and a red tie. And I think the idea of that would be they would not be allowed to go into pubs. This was understandable because, after all, if you are wounded you are sick and, if you went into a pub, the people there would be buying you drinks and this could have a detrimental effect. But it had good effect in this respect: if you went into a restaurant or you went into a shop then very often they wouldn't charge the lads for the tea or packet of cigarettes. But I always felt sorry for them because the uniforms were hideous.

First World War Peace Party, Westbourne Street, Hull, 1920.

[Christopher Ketchell Collection]

90

MRS McKERNON *[interviewed in Hull in 1982; no personal details available.]*

Smith and Nephew's was only a small place against the pier. They did the first field dressings in the First World War there. It was 4/6d a week if you were lucky because you had to do a 100 for 6d. The trays used to come in and there would be a khaki bandage, a piece of lint, a little bandage with a little piece of lint inside, a piece of gauze, a bandage and a safety pin. They used to come wrapped up from the machines down below — in a sort of waterproof wrapping. Then you put them in a tray. It took you all day to get 6d, so at the end of the week you didn't always get 4/6d. You might get 4 shillings because some were quicker than others.

Women also filled the shells down in Cannon Street at Rose, D owns and Thompson's. That was where the dummy gun was on the top, the wooden gun, with a soldier guarding it. My mother used to say, 'Go and see if the soldier's on the gun.' The bairns used to go by and say, 'Oh, yes. They're guarding the gun.' It was a wooden one. The place would have blown to blazes if a real gun had ever fired at a Zeppelin because it was an ammunition works. The women used to fill the shells. They didn't wear uniform. They wore dungarees.

MRS MACLEAN *[interviewed in Hull by Briege Devine in 1980; no personal details available for publication.]*

I was born in Manor Street. I used to go to school nearby. Then I went to school down Wansbeck Road. It was a great big school, boys down one side and us down the other. We were never mixed up. The boys were in the next yard. They couldn't come in the playground with us. The teacher would come round and watch us — we used to have skipping ropes and other things — and if anyone started fighting they would sort it out. Down the stairs at the end of the playground was a place where you could do some washing. You could take things from home and wash them.

We did writing and arithmetic. You stood all around the school and the teacher would tell you to spell different words, and if you couldn't spell the word you had to stop there till you knew it. Then you could go out. We used to go in the big hall to drill and we used to learn songs and sing with the piano. We had plays at Easter and Christmas and people came in to watch us.

In Manor Street there were two houses, a sweet shop, a boot maker and then a big shop that used to sell beer, cheese and treacle. You took a jar to get treacle because they kept it in big barrels, and you held your jar under the tap to fill it for just a few coppers. Everything was cheap then.

We had a big garden with four plum trees, two pear trees, a grape vine over the back of the house and we grew flowers and had a square for us to play on. We weren't allowed to go out in the street. The rest of the garden was for beans, potatoes, beetroots and the like. Down at the bottom of the garden was a chicken house. We kept chickens and when we had a lot of eggs I used to take them to the shop where I worked.

I went straight to the shop from leaving school. The shopkeeper used to have a woman working for him but I suppose she was going to get married or something, and when I went in there once to buy something he asked me how old I was, and I said I would be 14 soon and leaving school. 'Oh, well,' he said, 'That'll be alright. Don't go anywhere else, come here.' So there I was. I got about 3 shillings a week plus, of course, my food. He was an old man and I suppose he got to like me. He had a violin and I got one too so I could start playing and he gave me his violin when he died. Mine wasn't a very good one but when I went out he used to give me his violin to play with. Then two or three years later on he said did I want something, and I said yes. I had aunts and uncles who used to play mandolins, so he got me a mandolin. I went to a teacher to learn to play the violin and then, when the war was on and the soldiers were about and people were brought over with broken legs and bandages and all sorts, we used to go and play for them. We went to different places. I forget what they used to call them (soup kitchens? workhouses?) but we used to go in there. Someone asked us, 'What did you go in there for?' He thought we were poor people, you see. But they were all soldiers in there and we used to go in there and play for them, mandolins, violins, piano and the teacher would come with us as well — two or three men, two or three women. Some of the girls used to dance and show them how to do things.

One of the men boarders at my teacher's had heard us playing and asked her to take us over to France. He'd been in France I suppose. I was only about 12 or 13 years old. When I went home and told my father he said, 'You're not going over to France.' So I couldn't go. Well you never know what could have happened to us if we'd gone. I suppose they had men over there who had been poorly and he thought we'd be able to play for them.

It was very difficult to get food in the first war. My mother used to go to one shop and I would go to another and my sister (she was about 2 years younger than me) would go to another. Everybody had to do that, it was terrible. They had a job to get stuff into the shops, I think. The thing that was most short was butter. You could only get a bit of butter. I used to go along to the shop and my sister would be two or three behind me and we'd get two or three potatoes each. My mother went to the butcher's, and perhaps if we went to another one we might get something. We used to get bits and pieces all over. There weren't any ration books in the first war; people used to get things where they could.

MR HARRY ROWNTREE *[interviewed in 1985 at Wold Haven Home, Pocklington, by Maureen Fagan.]*

I was born at Middleton on the Wolds in 1893. When the war started in 1914, I was shepherd at North Dalton. I was shepherd there for twenty-two years.

That was when Sir Mark Sykes formed the Waggoners' Reserve. I knew a few of them. I knew one or two who went that night and we never saw them any more. They had been given a pound apiece to sign on and then they were to be ready if anything started. When the night came, they were called up and simply had to pack up their troubles and go. All young men of military age had to go, but I got exemption for being a shepherd. Even the master of the hounds went to the war.

Extracts from *Waggoners' Reserve* B.B.C. Radio Humberside Archive programme, produced by Trevor Austin.

'When I left school I was thirteen, fourteen in the April. I passed a labour exam and went to work on a farm at Great Kelk, just outside Driffield, tending pigs. I used to take a herd of pigs to the field on a morning and stop there and have my dinner in the field and bring them home every night.'

'We used to get all our clothes on a year's credit, you know. You used to go and get sixteen yards of shirting, Oxford shirting, and lining, and flannelette for under-shirting, and me sisters and me mother used to be sewing all Martinmas week, fit for you to go back. And you used to go for a "sub", during the year, and they wanted to know what you wanted it for, you know ... you'd think you'd asked for the farm. I got to be a waggoner and I was single foreman when I went into the army at Mr. Winter's at Manor Farm, Middleton-on-the-Wolds.'

'I was waggoner at Huggate Wold — head horseman — and we took what they called the silly pound. There was heaps of them taking this here pound, which was a lot of money then. Colonel Sir Mark Sykes (of Sledmere House) held meetings at Middleton, Driffield and Bridlington.'

'You were tied for a year. No exercises, no training, but a driving competition at Sledmere Bottom. I won it. Sykes had told Lord Kitchener he could get him a thousand skilled drivers to drive heavy horses in pole waggons in the army, and he could get them at ten minutes' notice. And Kitchener allowed him to get them.'

'The 6th of August, very early morning, their papers came. The policeman saw them on to the train, and some fellows always boozed, and they tell me some of them got tight, and they took them to Middleton Station on a handcart and pushed them into the carriages.'

'I called back at farm and told them I was going, I'd got me papers, and I went down, and first pub I came to I said, 'Can I leave me bike here, I'm off to war.' When we got to Bradford we got rigged up with clothes — they threw a tunic at you, and breeches, and puttees, and a bandoleer, and last of all a rifle. You had to look after that — you had to pay for it if you lost it.'

'All the waggoners had to mobilise at Bradford Moor Barracks. We were first into France in supply columns. Eventually we were posted into different infantry regiments, and lost one another.'

'After a year's service you could come out, or sign on for the duration. I signed on — twenty pounds down and twenty pounds at the end of the war.' *[Waggoners saw action at Le Cateau, Mons and other Western Front battlefields.]* 'I didn't mind it — it was hard, and there was more danger, but it was hard being a horseman on a farm in any case.'